INFLUENCE
NEGOTIATE
WIN

INFLUENCE NEGOTIATE WIN

The Only Negotiation Book
You Will Ever Need When
Negotiating For Success

ABHISHEK DATTA

Influence Negotiate Win
Author: Abhishek Datta
Email: datta.ab@gmail.com

Published in **Kolkata, India**
Published by Abhishek Datta

ISBN 978-93-5407-000-6
Copyright © Abhishek Datta, 2020

All rights reserved. No part of this publication may be reproduced, stored in or introduced into a retrieval system, or transmitted, in any form, or by any means (electrical, mechanical, photocopying, recording or otherwise) without the prior written permission of the author or publisher.

This publication is sold subject to the condition that it shall not, by way of trade or otherwise, be lent, resold, hired out, or otherwise circulated without the authors' prior consent in any form of binding or cover other than that in which it is published and without a similar condition including this condition being imposed on the subsequent purchaser. Under no circumstances may any part of this book be photocopied for resale.

Any person who does any unauthorised act in relation to this publication may be liable to criminal prosecution and civil claims for damages.

This book is dedicated to the indomitable spirit of individuals who strive to better themselves and the lives of others around them.

Contents

Introduction	*1*
Neediness	*15*
Build the Bridge	*32*
Void your Mind	*48*
Active Listening	*64*
Dynamic Silence	*85*
Dig Deeper	*98*
NO is Music	*116*
Focus Questions	*134*
Time Tales	*152*
Influencing Strategies	*171*
Price is just a Perception	*193*
Appendix	*211*
Acknowledgement	*216*

Knowing your negotiation style is important in business and in life. However, knowing that of your counterpart is crucial to your success as a negotiator. All readers can now access the Negotiation Styles Handbook free of charge. To claim yours, please email to datta.ab@gmail.com

INTRODUCTION

The gift of a good negotiator is making people believe that you lack a talent for negotiating.

I was perched on the edge of a luxurious leather sofa waiting to meet Mr. Singh. It was the office of one of the largest conglomerates in the country, located on the top floor of a twenty-storied building overlooking a scenic view of the city. My meeting with Mr. Gurpreet Singh was scheduled in couple of minutes. He headed the Channel Sales and Distribution for the Eastern Region. After an exemplary MBA from India's top Business School, he had joined the conglomerate eight years back as a Business Development Manager. Since then, he had zoomed fast through the ranks and was recently promoted as the Vice President (East) for a wide portfolio of products. Being one of the youngest VPs in the conglomerate, he had received multiple awards and was recently conferred with a swanky lavish corner office.

On the other hand, I was responsible for channel distribution for a line of products for this conglomerate. As a mid-sized distribution organization, we would purchase from them and use our distribution channels to supply the products to retailers across the state. Our network across the state was one of the best and we could deliver products efficiently and quickly to any retailer even at the remotest of places. It was going comfortably as planned till suddenly everything turned topsy-turvy. The economic downturn hit very hard and the market started drying up. This resulted in a pile of stocks which we could neither sell nor liquidate. The products were dumped in a warehouse, rusting. Buyers were dwindling and those who bought had far exceeded their credit limits.

Everything was at stake.

You have heard of the phrase "Cash is King." Our problem was that the market did not have cash. Retailers we catered to could not sell to the end customers. And those who bought the products could not pay upfront. Credits had maxed out. Money was stuck in stocks and rolling had stopped. The market had crashed and we were facing an imminent danger of liquidity.

But there was an even more challenging problem. Mr. Singh was about to force us to buy more stocks to meet his monthly and annual target. What would translate to him in terms of a hefty year-end bonus would literally devastate us and bring us to down on our knees. It was an all-out war – not physical but a war of the minds.

Stakes were high. We have to take a stand. The question was how to take a stand without hurting his ego. After all, we would need him when the economy looks up. It was a full-on negotiation coming up.

I heard my name called out by Mr. Singh's secretary. Stood up and made my way into his cabin.

GAMES PEOPLE PLAY

Some negotiators have fake win-win pasted all over their demeanor. A smile on the face, a bit of nudge to find a mid-way solution to problems and a handshake to close the deal. Win-win means that all parties in the negotiation gets something out of the deal. That is what we have been taught all through. We have been taught to take the middle path in a negotiation or a deal. Let both parties win. Let both parties compromise a bit to get to an agreement. In fact, going all out to capture the entire pie in the negotiation is against our values and ethics. A shared success is an optimal one. It feels good. It feels right.

Fundamentally, there are two approaches to negotiation. The first is called Partner Approach where all parties involved in the negotiation work collaboratively to maximize everyone's value. The second is called the Positional Approach where each party takes a positon or a stand and bargains hard to split the pie in their favor. Many pundits and books teach us to drop all thoughts of positional negotiation because it hurts the final outcome and urges us to focus on win-win all the time.

A Partner Approach is a win-win approach. All parties come to the table, lay out their stands and asks, discusses openly about how to proceed to ensure everybody wins and makes a decision. In a Partner Approach, all parties freely share their objectives, limitations and requirements and work on idea generation. But do you see the catch here? The catch is the word "freely" and the fact that each party can be trusted to share their actual objectives in the negotiations. Really?

Let me tell you this. Someone who explicitly preaches "win-win" has something fishy going on. Playing win-win without knowing how you stack up against your counterpart's *reality* is like entering the slaughterhouse. In practice, it is going to get you killed. Most seasoned negotiators who preach win-win are playing a win-lose game. It is you who is going to lose. Win-win is a master negotiation tool deployed by experts to deal with people naïve enough to think that they are up against a fair opponent.

Think of win-win as this. You are visiting an optical store with your spouse to get a pair of contact lens. The store salesperson shows you a lot of options. You want something with a tint of color but you are confused with the colour choices. You glance at your spouse and ask the question. You like the honey brown colour – it goes with your personality. Your spouse feels that the grey one suits you better. What do you do? If you think win-win, you would wear a honey brown on one eye and a grey lens on the other eye every day. How does that sound? Ridiculous, right? That's win-win for you. Everybody wins. But the final outcome is worse than either of the other outcomes.

Let me demonstrate you with another example. Suppose there is an event going on – a very popular event where you can get hundreds of eyeballs of your most desired customer base. The event organizers propose to sell you a stall for INR 8 Lakhs. You feel that if you can negotiate with the organizers and get the deal at INR 7 Lakhs, that would be great. The organizers explain to you about the footfalls expected and that they have given you the lowest possible deal. They have given you a win-win deal, they say. So, you negotiate with the organizers and get yourself a deal at INR 7 Lakhs. You are absolutely elated. You feel it is a great win-win deal. You have just saved INR 1 Lakh simply through negotiation. So, you take the deal and go home happy. But, few days later, you come to know that the same organizers have sold a similar stall space for just INR 1 Lakh to someone else. Do you then think yours was a win-win deal? Your perspective just changed. Didn't it?

Take another example. You are in an interview. It is a good company and they are offering a package of INR 20 Lakhs. This is about 25% more than your previous salary. Do you take it? What if another employee in the company with same experience and same profile is getting INR 23 Lakhs? Did you just lose out?

Anyone running a small business or representing a small business knows how few large clients squeeze you out on every deal – right from pricing to terms of payment. You would be pitched against competitors, played hardball and forced into negotiating on unfair terms, or made to work on wafer-thin margins. And anybody who has been through this situation knows that you can neither accept nor refuse the offer. Many offer deals with sky-high targets that you cannot meet and you get screwed with late fines. Or just when you have made the purchase of the raw materials for your production, they cancel the deal only to return few weeks later to re-negotiate the contract on much meaner terms. Do you think they are playing win-win here? Your and your employees' families are on the line, but your counterpart negotiator would probably be winning a trophy for being the Best Manager.

Debraj Mukherjee, a friend of mine recollected this incident. He runs a placement service agency catering to businesses across India. When he started out about 15 years back, he received an offer from a mid-sized firm to recruit 35 people over the course of one year. The firm told him that given the size of the offer, they must chalk out a "win-win" plan so that both parties benefitted. They convinced Debraj to lower his recruitment charges and they would make Debraj one of the prime recruitment agencies for the firm.

Once the charges were negotiated, the firm came back after few days saying there has been a sudden hiring freeze. And as per firm's latest policies, they would want to recruit only couple of candidates. And that they would feel offended if Debraj declined the offer.

"I have never been in such a bind before. It was new to me. We did the job to save the relationship but made almost nothing out of the deal." He confided in me. "Next time, I hear someone throw that bait, my guards go up drastically."

Win-win is a brainwash. The best negotiators I have seen and worked with are skeptical of anyone who tries the win-win phrase. It is meant for the gullible. In this book, we are going to look at negotiations in a different light. In only a handful of negotiations, you can have an estimate of what seems to be a good deal. An example of this would be visiting your local market. You go around 4-5 shops, get an estimate of the average price for items and buy. However, in most negotiations, there would be not enough data to decide what is the best price to close the deal. You would have a broad estimate, but there wouldn't be a way to narrow down the target price. For example, purchasing a software, buying a used car, asking for a salary raise or renting out a property. What do you do then? How do you get to negotiate when you don't know your opponent's cards?

Coming back to my visit to Mr. Singh's office. I walked into his swanky corner office. Along with him were four other members from the Conglomerate. Pressure tactics, you know.

Mr. Singh said, "Welcome Mr. Datta. How are you doing?"

I feigned a sweet smile on my face. I knew what I was getting into.

"How are you doing?" I said. And then looked at the other four members and smiled profusely. Inside, my stomach was in knots. That is a feeling that I have come to terms with. Whenever I get into negotiations even now, I can feel that tightening in my stomach. Probably a good sign – that I am not too confident to be reckless. Something that can keep me on my toes. You know what's worse than a bad negotiation? A negotiation where you never knew what hit you. That's why I feel assured when my stomach tightens.

Mr. Singh: "Would you like some tea?" With the tea called for, we got down to business.

He started, "We see that your company is way behind the target numbers in terms of sales. You had been doing well for the first two quarters this year, but there is a huge dip in business in the last two quarters. We were expecting a much larger sales figure possibly exceeding your target numbers."

Over the years, I had picked up skills to negate the effects of anchoring. I smiled and stared at Mr. Singh, effectively asking him to continue.

Introduction

Mr. Singh: "You know this is the Financial Year end and such low numbers would make you and your company look unpromising to our Senior Management. Our senior management always had high regards for you. However, with such low numbers, they might have to revisit their thoughts. There have been cases where such low number led to termination of the contract. But, I know you well personally. We don't want that to happen and I am here to help you. Let's make this a win-win situation here. You are short of your target by INR 25 Lakhs. Why don't you make a purchase for this amount by this month-end and we will work out some discounts for you?"

I smiled again. I just saw what he did. First anchoring and expectation setting, then playing the ally, win-win stroke, anchoring again and finally the reciprocity game. But that wasn't going to bend me. He was playing a game. It was time to beat him at this own game. With this economic scenario, it would be better if we could return some of the existing stocks back to them. There is no point in purchasing even a single rupee worth of items.

I looked at Mr. Singh and said in a sincere tone, "We really appreciate you taking time out for the discussion. We also have immense respect for our relationship and always look forward to working with you. I am sorry but with the current economic scenario, I am not sure how I can purchase more."

Mr. Singh paused, slightly perturbed as if something felt wrong. He had a look of pity on his face. It was as if I was requesting him to help me out. He collected his thoughts and pressed on, "The current till-date numbers are very low for you. There is a target that we had set at the beginning of the year, and you have to honor the target. You have to pick up INR 25 Lakhs worth of goods by this month-end."

I waited for him to stop. And said in a sincere deep voice, "We don't have money to cover our expenses as the goods are not moving in this economic scenario. Money is stuck in credits and stocks. In such case, we were thinking of returning some of the existing stocks to you. Please help me understand how can I pick up more stocks."

I had just countered his argument with an apology, a counter-anchor and a focus question. The discussion had pivoted from not making sales number to how Mr. Singh can help us cover our expenses. It was as if we had made Mr. Singh an ally in figuring out how he can solve the expenses puzzle for my company. In other words, I had Mr. Singh trying to figure out my problems.

Mr. Singh looked bemused. Something had struck him, but he wasn't sure what. Shifting uneasily in his chair, he turned to his colleagues for support. He paused for a minute, flipped the pen in his hand a couple of times and then said, "Let us come back to you in few days."

The war wasn't over, but I had won this battle. INR 25 Lakhs saved.

COAXING VS COMPELLING

Negotiation is about coaxing your counterpart to give you what you want. Not compelling but coaxing. Coaxing is requesting. Coaxing is asking. Coaxing is nudging. Coaxing is respecting your counterpart for who they are. The best negotiations are those where the counterpart walks away happy after giving you what you need.

If at any point during the negotiating, your counterpart feels violated or compelled to do something, it is going to backfire. The relationship will suffer or your counterpart will backtrack from whatever they had agreed to. Human beings need to feel safe and comfortable to be able to open up. Most negotiations are long-term in nature, either with the same vendor or the same client or the same set of people. You wouldn't want to destroy the relationship over one negotiation and rule out possibilities of future talks. And that will happen only if your counterpart feels respected.

I was once taking a session on negotiation. There was a point on the slide which read "The best negotiation is one where your counterpart assures himself that your ask is what he always wanted."

A participant walks up to me and says "Well, I don't agree to your point. All I care for is that I get what I want. I don't care whether the counterpart is compelled to give it to me or not." He was coming from the view of a transactional one-time negotiation, like one with a random street hawker. But most negotiations are not like that. Ninety percent of the people we negotiate with would be one with whom we would expect a long term relationship. Like a business with their clients, a mother with her child, a boss with his employees or one country with another. You wouldn't want to destroy the relationship.

I replied with an example, "Think that you are negotiating with your boss on salary raise. You tell your boss that you have got an offer from a competitor organization for 25%. You will stay in the role only if your boss matches the offer. What does he do? He smiles and agrees to your demand. And after few weeks, he recruits someone else and fires you from the role. That is compelling someone to agree to your demands."

"If on the other hand," I continued, "you discussed the entire issue with your boss highlighting your asks empathetically, he would have given you the same increment and you would have saved your job."

WHAT YOU CAN EXPECT FROM THIS BOOK?

Selling to clients. Asking for a raise. Building a new relationship. Saying No to someone. Navigating difficult customers. Putting across a contradicting viewpoint to a majority. Apologizing to angry customers. Bargaining for the best price. Dealing with gatekeepers. Getting your kids to sleep. Deciding on the holiday destination with your spouse. Negotiation is everywhere. At home or office. You cannot avoid negotiation. Wherever there are people involved, negotiations are bound to happen.

Negotiation is a tricky concept in countries that follow social hierarchy. People can bargain hard in common everyday scenario, but find it difficult to express themselves in negotiations with people who are looking to build long term relations or with people senior in age and designation. They are quite direct in the former cases. For the latter, however, an indirect ambiguous style is used to show respect; politeness, disagreement, refusal, or avoid confrontation. This construct comes out of the upbringing of most people where one has been brought up to obey rather than to question.

I draw from experiences in my life and career, both from failures and successes, and outline here what works and what doesn't. Over more than a decade and a half, I have been part of thousands of negotiations either in personal or professional spheres. From financial bargaining to non-monetary negotiations, from emotional counterparts to logical ones and from dominating asks to begging requests, I have seen a gamut of ways negotiations play out. No two negotiations are same, but there is an undercurrent that consistently flows across all interactions. That is the human psyche. If there is one constant factor that persistently makes a difference, it is the understanding of how human psychology plays out in the compass of negotiations.

As a child, I have been always shy of negotiations and could not vocalize what I wanted while growing up. Over a period of time and after exposure to different cultures and mindsets, I have found that negotiation is not about talking or forcing your counterpart to give in to your demands. Rather than compelling them, it is more of a coaxing process – nudging your counterpart slowly in the direction you want them to move.

People are averse to negotiations in general. They would rather give in than negotiating for what's right and what's theirs. But that need not always be true from now on. As you read the book see that negotiation is nothing more than communication on steroids. It is a way of discussing with your counterpart and looking at common ways to solve your problems.

Introduction

This book is a culmination of my journey so far, dealing with individuals across business and life in general. With the skills that I have learned, I found that these are easy to implement once we know the what and the how – what techniques to use and how to implement those techniques.

This book is written like you are watching a thriller movie. In a thriller movie, the detective starts by looking at the available evidence, then explores further unearthing more information, then uses techniques to get deeper into the mystery, then gets into the inevitable core and finally ends by putting together all of the puzzles into a coherent explanation for the audience to understand. Similarly, in this book, you will start probing slowly from what is visible, then use sharp techniques to dig deeper into negotiations, then get into hard bargains and finally end by how you can put together all the learnings from the book into real-life negotiations.

Each chapter starts with a real-life story, setting the ground for using the negotiation tools. Then it moves into what worked and what didn't and the techniques that got used to deliver the results. We then discuss the principles behind the tools and show you different practical scenarios where these tools have been and can be successfully deployed to get results.

In the following chapter that is, Chapter 2, you will learn the ground rules for getting into any negotiation – the absolute fundamentals before starting any negotiation. This chapter covers the concept of Need versus Want and how negotiators unknowingly fall into the trap even before the negotiation starts. You will learn how to get over Neediness and the right way to approach negotiations.

Chapter 3 gives you the tools to build the bridge and start the negotiations process. You will learn how to make an impression which makes the negotiation process easier both for first time discussions as well as for repeated negotiations; and ways to use humor, apology and the *not-perfect* style to build rapport with the counterpart.

In Chapter 4, you will see how to void your mind to prevent yourself from sabotaging the negotiations. You will get to know how expectations and assumptions play a vital role in deciding negotiation outcomes and how to tune your mind like the radar to pick up all signals that come from the counterpart.

Chapter 5 gets into active listening using words, tone of voice and body language. Learn how to get your counterpart speaking with mirroring, flipping and blocking techniques and get them to divulge more and more information that you can use later in the negotiations process.

In Chapter 6, learn about one of the most aggressive tools in a negotiator's arsenal – the dynamic silence and how to use it correctly to win over arguments without even talking. Talking is not always necessary to win negotiations when silence can do the deal.

Chapter 7 deals with how to resonate with the counterpart and making them feel comfortable and secure to let down their guards. Hack into System 1 thinking of the counterpart's mind and use the rehash and acknowledge technique to make inroads into deeper why behind their asks.

In Chapter 8, learn to breakdown the counterpart's barriers and resistance using No-oriented discussions. You will get to know how to use No as a tool to cut through to the core and unmask their objections; plus, learn how to deal with ultimatums and 'take it or leave it' mindset.

Chapter 9 deals with focus questions and how you can use them to get your counterparts to expend their energy into giving you what you want. Learn to use interrogative questioning with What, How and Why along with a softening phrase to make it look like a request for help.

In Chapter 10, learn to amplify your counterpart's time costs and get them invested in the deal. Use deadline pressure to let them hasten their negotiation and make concessions, learn to work with gatekeepers and blockers and how to vet the negotiation process to save time.

Chapter 11 deals with influencing strategies meant to nudge your counterpart to see your side of the story and persuade them to take action. These are psychological tools to make your offer seemingly reasonable and coax your counterpart to give you what you want.

In Chapter 12, you will learn the inevitable discussions around Price Negotiations and Financial bargaining and how to use the principles from the earlier chapters to make a coherent strategy to get to the price you want to pay for or sell at. Also, learn how to pilot Salary discussions and have your boss give you the hike that you want.

Appendix A deals with Sales Negotiation Checklist providing a summary of steps you need to take before and after getting into a sales discussion with your customers.

The beauty of negotiation is that it helps you reach your goals for business or personal happiness in a faster and quicker way while at the same time building and nurturing relationship with your counterpart. Negotiation has been eye-opening for me in my life and has made my life more meaningful. More than just an art-form, negotiation has a lot of science and technique behind it, which makes it easier to learn and faster to implement. Rather than searching in the dark for answers for why (or why don't) somethings work, use the techniques in this book to make life simpler.

With that said, let us deep dive into the world of negotiations. It is a wonderful journey and one where you will learn to navigate the human psychology, unearth the true reasons why someone is asking for what they are demanding, make connections with your counterpart and above all enjoy the process. When you finish the book, it would mean a lot for me if you can use these techniques in your life either in business negotiations or personal negotiations to improve your career or life in general.

And lastly I would like to ask you a question. Would it be a horrible idea to request you to send me some of your success stories having implemented the techniques laid out in the book? The best ones will be published in our blogs and case studies sections.

Every day is negotiation – it just depends on how you look at it.

Everyone is a born negotiator.

You too can negotiate.

Abhishek Datta April 2020

Email: datta.ab@gmail.com

NEEDINESS

It was my twentieth interview. I was sitting in a row with nine other students waiting for my turn to walk into the interview room. My mouth was running dry and legs were shaking. With the nauseating summer heat and the cringing tension of the upcoming grilling session, nervous sweat ran down the face. My crisp white shirt went from dry to moist to sticky. The handkerchief was dripping wet and the socks were smelling from the sweat. Somewhere outside another interview room, I heard fellow students high-fiving – they had just cracked an interview. Pressure was mounting with every passing moment. The earlier nineteen companies had rejected me. I was desperate to get an internship.

It was those fateful Summer Internship interviews that was taking place in my MBA College. Ours was one of the finest MBA Colleges in the country where thousands applied every year and only a few got through. Taught by the best minds in the country, it was what any student would die for. Our college had alumni in numerous high-profile positions across the globe and every year companies would line up to select students for internships or final placements.

"Number 1," called the Interview-in-Charge. Off went the first student to the interview room. I was third in line.

What had started off as an optimistic affair had turned into a hauntingly inexorable nightmare. One after the other, companies were rejecting me. The excitement of striding into the corporate world had soon turned into a helpless burden of anxiety and fear. My mind was racing. Veins were throbbing on the sides of my head. What if this company rejected me? What if I get rejected again? What should I tell my parents who were spending their hard-earned money to get me through MBA? I hadn't still told them about my earlier rejects. It was humiliating and disgraceful. It would have been better to take up the low-paying job after graduation. Why did I even bother to get into an MBA college? An MBA was probably not my cup of tea. If this company rejected me, I would not be able to show my face to my friends or family. I was desperate to get selected.

"Number 2," called the Interview-in-Charge. I hadn't noticed that fifteen long minutes had passed. The first student came out from the interview room visibly shaken. He stared at the rest of us, swept his index finger across his throat signaling that he just got slaughtered in the interview.

A well-known FMCG company was interviewing for the sales and marketing role. It was one of the most coveted internship profile in the company. One that could lead to a permanent placement offer and with that launch me into an illustrious career. It came not only with a massive stipend but also gave a substantial opportunity to learn and have first-hand experience in applying marketing principles to real-life scenarios. This internship would also open up networking access to the entire senior management team at the company. I needed this internship. The interviews I had given in the earlier companies were across a mix of profiles - finance, marketing, supply chain and operations. But what did I care? I needed to get into any company that would take me. I even didn't want a stipend for the internship. I simply wanted to save face and tell my parents that I got through.

"Number 3," called the Interview-in-Charge, pointing at me. I took a slow deep breath. I needed to crack the interview. I needed to get selected. My heartbeat skyrocketed through the roof. I stood up, but my mind sat back down. My ears got warmer and my palms sweated copiously. Rubbing my palms on the side of my trousers, I dragged myself to the interview room.

YOU DON'T *NEED* A DEAL

Human beings are attuned to pick up signs of neediness. We have a natural instinct to detect neediness in other human beings. A crying baby often takes advantage of the mother's neediness – the need to keep her baby protected. A buyer who bargains hard with a roadside vegetable vendor for INR 1 discount takes advantage of the fact that vegetables are perishable. More often than not, human beings, take advantage of the needy and the vulnerable. Or, in a not-so-grim restatement, become skeptical of the person showing neediness. In your life as a negotiator, you would often come across people who, like predators, are looking out for signs of weakness in you. The moment they sense a need in you, the predator in them starts salivating.

When was the last time you bought an item from a salesperson who had given an unbelievable discount?

"Here is something that we usually sell for INR 1000, but today we are giving it off at INR 100."

Are you skeptical of the person or the product quality?

What is the first thing that crosses your mind? "Why is the product being offered at such low prices?" "Are people not buying it at all?" "Surely something is wrong." And then you probe deeper.

"Need" are things that you cannot live without, like food, clothing and shelter; which is something that everyone reading this book already has. You can add few more items to the "need" list but it differs from people to people, like basic intellectual and emotional security –love, family, friendship, satisfying work, basic income, faith, hobbies, and the like. Everything else is "want". Desperation or need manifests in different forms. The obvious demonstration of neediness is an excessive willingness to please, to do just *any* deal or agree to the terms of the counterpart. Know someone who brags? That's also desperation. So is too much of table-thumping, impoliteness or disproportionate show of anger. In other words, such behavior shows how emotionally attached you are to the outcome. Both ends of the spectrum – excessive willingness or excessive anger – will often lead to outcomes detrimental to you.

If there is only one thing that you can take from this book, it is the concept of Need versus Want versus Nice-to-have. In today's world, we are not needy. We simply are not. There are enough alternatives. Even then, we hear terms like:

"I need this deal."

"I need this car."

"I need to get the distributorship." Or,

"I need this job."

Need often translates into fear and we start losing focus on the broader perspective. If we cannot control this fear, our performance at the negotiation table drops drastically.

Waiting to know what happened to my twentieth Summer Internship Interview? You would have guessed it by now. I dragged myself into the interview room, desperate to get the internship.

"Good Afternoon," I said shakily, my voice betrayed my desperation.

"Good Afternoon. Have a seat," one of the interviewers pulled out my CV from the pile in front of him and started probing, "You seem quite tensed. Why don't we start with your graduation project here?" He started asking me a variety of questions.

Though I can't recall exactly what I was answering, but what I can recall is myself fumbling, searching for answers, wiping the sweat off my forehead and sporadic moments of ghost-quiet silence. This went on for some time and then I remember this one question he asked, "How many interviews did you attend before this?"

With my mind struggling to deal with the fear of rejection, I blurted out without thinking, "Nineteen," and then added, "Sir, I need this internship."

And I am pretty sure to this day, that this one sentence had done me in. Companies do not hire you because you need the job. They hire you because they need your expertise. And a marketing guy who cannot control his neediness would never make the cut.

As dreaded, I got rejected.

Need externalizes through a range of behavior.

Take this example of an apparent display of neediness by John Forbes Kerry, an American politician who ran as the Democratic nominee in the 2004 presidential election but lost to Republican President George W. Bush. In January 2013, Kerry was confirmed to be the Secretary of State during President Barack Obama's second term and assumed the office on February 1, 2013. Kerry was known for his hands-on approach to solving problems. He was energetic and was not afraid to get his hands dirty, be it taking control of the Iran nuclear deal or negotiations in the Middle East. Here is an assessment of John Kerry's negotiating style as chronicled in international media.

Kerry had been flying to key hotspots around the world in an attempt to ensure his mark in the global political scene. In the negotiations with Iran, he reportedly seized the role of lead US negotiator (replacing Wendy Sherman) to do a deal. And, in the process revealed his desperation and neediness to strike *any* deal for that matter.

As negotiators, we often meet with counterparts who try too hard, such as salespeople who pester us with phone calls or overwhelms us with messages. Their desperation becomes clear leading us to question their commitment to their objectives and in turn leaving them open to getting crushed. Often they would have lost their leverage on the discussion and would agree to any deal which gets them to save face. The New York Times reported that Kerry was eager to meet his Iranian counterpart Md Javad Zarif anywhere in the world, including Geneva, Paris, Davos, Lausanne, Montreux, Munich, and New York City. It was as if he was chasing the deal and clearly displayed a sense of neediness from his side to reach a conclusion.

Finally, to get the deal, he bestowed significant power and leverage to Iran ignoring key US interests.

In most major negotiations, having the top leader at the table is, in itself, a sign of how much the deal means to you. While this is not uncommon for high-stakes negotiations, it gives too much control to your counterpart and often leads to the counterpart feeling that they can get away with much more than anticipated. And when your counterpart senses this desperation, he turns into a predator. Tough negotiators are master in sensing need in adversaries and often are experts in creating a sense of neediness.

HOW TO OVERCOME NEEDINESS

The single biggest obstacle in the path to overcoming neediness is the fear of rejection. We are afraid of not getting what we want. Be it business dealings, job interviews or relationships, people portray their sweeter side to get liked. Uncomfortable realities are coated with false smiles or niceness. Or on the other extreme, anger is used to cloud judgement. The truth is that you are not needy. You do not need that deal or that job. There are other deals and other jobs. There is no point

Neediness

in sacrificing too much to get to where you want. Remember win-win which we discussed in the earlier chapter. This is a compromise to get to a place where your interests are sacrificed. A bad deal is worse than no deal.

Nothing kills you. I repeat, nothing kills you. That is what you have to understand. A crucial thing to realize is that you cannot get rejected by someone if you don't want to. Only you have the power to reject yourself. That's it. Nobody else can reject you. To give someone else the power to reject you is to give them power over you. Never allow them to do so or even to believe that they do.

To become a solid negotiator, you have to get rid of the neediness. You need to be able to walk away from deals that you don't like.

Take this common example. You are bargaining in the grocery market. If negotiations with the vendor does not materialize, you walk away. Two things happen – either the vendor agrees to an even lower price; or he doesn't. If he agrees with your price, you take the deal. If he doesn't, you probably would find an alternate vendor or alternate recipe for the day.

Large manufacturing houses often use the fear of rejection against their channel partners. They pitch one channel partner against the other, getting them to act against their own interests. That is neediness on part of both the partners. If each partner realizes this and walks away from the deal, then none of them would have to fight it out. A show of neediness also triggers the suspicion of the counterpart. Why is someone getting too needy? It makes them feel uncomfortable and probes them to look deeper into the deal.

At the negotiating table, you must avoid showing signs of need. How? Find out alternatives (which we will discuss in later chapters). You do not need any deal. There is always another one coming up. I will share how not being needy helped me.

Post the Summer Internship debacle, I tried to find out ways to remove the desperation. I realized that my neediness stemmed from the fear of rejection and what it meant to my impending career. I sat down one day and listed out alternate routes I can take if I don't get a job from the campus.

One could be applying out of campus.

Two, taking up a lower salary job at my hometown.

Three, applying for further studies.

Four, the number of job offers given in the campus far exceeded the number of students, so anyways some company would take me.

And so on. I did a list of fourteen alternatives if a campus job didn't materialize.

The result of so much thinking? In my final placements the following year, I got through three companies on the first day of the placement season. And this I attribute to one single fact – the fact that I wasn't needy. Yes, I wanted a job. It was nice to get a job at a good company. But I wasn't needy. The fear of rejection was completely gone. It helped me become more composed, think clearly and last but not the least gave off a very positive vibe in the interview sessions. For all of you who are applying to jobs or looking for a job change, get neediness out of the way. Even if you are without a job currently.

A big disadvantage of small businesses is their willingness to sell at discounted prices. This issue is particularly prominent in Service Industry and for self-employed professionals where there isn't a standard measure to benchmark cost. In a desperation to get business, services are offered at unsustainable prices. A friend of mine runs a web design firm. In this interconnected economy, his competition is not only from local players, but from freelancers and companies across the globe. In a bid to get customers, he started offering services 50% to 60% below standard rates. It got him immediate results and he picked up a few clients.

There is a folklore about a frog put into tepid water which is then slowly brought to boil. The frog does not notice the gradual change in the temperature, but by the time it feels the heat, it is too incapacitated and burnt to escape. Same was the situation for the web design company. Initially for the first few weeks it enjoyed the back to back clients it got because of the low pricing. He grasped the damage this pricing strategy had done when he figured out that his cost of running the business (including rent, salary, electricity costs, and the like) was way more than the price quoted to his clients. The low pricing could not justify his expenses leave aside profit.

Our neediness to get deals often leads us down paths that are detrimental in the long run. It is not that my friend did not understand this basic concept. But more often than not, our eagerness to close deals blinds us from obvious facts. He realized this soon and hiked up his prices. Well, then you can ask me, did he not lose clients to the competition. To answer the question, yes he did. But for one, he picked up more profitable clients which he could serve better and get a profit. And secondly, he started offering more value for the price he charged. We will come to the concept of perceived value and how to bargain on monetary terms in the later chapters.

NEEDINESS CAN KILL YOU

We were once approached by a listing website for a business we run. Listing websites or directories are platforms for business to list their services along with other businesses in similar domains. They categorize business by their industry, range of expertise and geographic locations. The listings on these websites help in visibility for small and medium businesses and generate leads for their business. On top of that the web directories also perform Search Engine Optimization to ensure that any searches on specific categories will show the most relevant companies in that category catering to the searcher's preferred location. The listing websites charge a fee to these businesses for getting featured near the top of the list. Often, these are cheaper than other methods of advertisement.

Akbar, representing a web directory, had been calling me up for the past few months now. Every time, either we ignored him or offered to meet him at a later date, which somehow we couldn't keep. He would send me messages and emails following up with me for a chance to explain the deal. It was not that we did not want the deal. We haven't said no to him. Every time he called, we asked him a new question about their services to keep the fire in him burning. We were waiting for a sweeter deal to come up. Usually around month-ends and specifically around year-ends, most companies in a bid to meet their targets offer deep discounted products. March is the financial year-end for most companies in India.

Around the second week of March, he called again. I picked up the call. His desperation to close the deal was very obvious from his voice. He was almost pleading over the phone to get the deal.

I asked him, "I am looking to start the service. However, the price is on the higher side. This is something that is beyond my budget."

Akbar pleaded, "Sir, what price are you looking for? It's year-ending and this deal will help me close my target." I had him on my side. Almost.

"I was looking for something on the lower side," I said, "You should be having discounts around this time." We didn't quote an expected price. We wanted to see how low he can get.

Akbar came back two days later, "Sir, I spoke to my manager. He could give a discount of 25% on the deal."

"This is year-end for us too. We do not have that amount of Cash left for spending. Can you check if you can give a better discount?" I said, still not quoting our expected discount. We wanted him to come down as much as possible and then we could start the bargaining process.

Neediness

Akbar hung up the phone. Then called me back in an hour. "Sir, I checked with my manager again. He can do 40% immediately," Bingo. I was overjoyed. I almost closed because this was a good deal. But sensing the desperation in his voice, I was tempted to go a bit further.

"That is a good deal, but still beyond my budget. If you can get me a 50% discount, I will write a cheque for the full amount by tomorrow."

Akbar muted his phone. Probably his manager was standing beside him listening to the conversation. He had a target to achieve. We wanted to get the best deal we could.

Akbar released the mute and sighed, "Yes, Sir, I will do it at 50%."

The only person who is okay to be needy is your counterpart. If you ever feel needy in a negotiation, take a step back. Need will kill you. Always be willing to walk away.

NO NEED TO BEAT THE COUNTERPART

You would never want to beat the counterpart just for the sake of negotiation. All negotiations that you get into will require you to have a goal. This goal is what would drive you to do the negotiations in full faith. When I say goal, it is not about getting the absolute lowest possible price or getting the most out of your customer. For example, if you are pitching to the customer and you are negotiating for a price, your ask is to ensure that you can deliver the best quality at that price. Any significant erosion of that price will compel you to compromise on the work. Will a compromised work be good for your customer? No. Would a compromised work be good for you? No. And it goes without saying that you wouldn't get any referrals.

This point may look conflicting to the previous negotiation with Akbar. But if you look closely, neither of us lost the negotiation. My goal was to ensure that we get a deal that will be financially prudent for our company. Akbar's goal was to make an additional sale before the year-end. Though he might not have got the deal of his lifetime, he was definitely inches closer to his target. The goal of this negotiation was not to negotiate just for the sake of negotiation. Each of us had our goals and we wanted to converge at a common point.

Look at this famous experiment. The experimenter pulls out an INR 2000 note and tells a group of participants to bid for the INR 2000 note. The starting bid will be INR 100 and will increase in multiples of INR 100. The final highest bidder will get the INR 2000 by paying the bid amount. There is only one caveat – the second-highest bidder will also have to pay the amount that he or she bids, but will obviously not get the INR 2000 note. For example, if the highest bidders are Person A (INR 500) and Person B (INR 400), then person A pays INR 500 and gets INR 2000. Person B pays the experimenter INR 400.

How do you think the bidding goes? The first person bids INR 100, the next person bids 200 and it starts. Very soon, the bids reach about INR 1000 – INR 1200 levels around which most participants back off leaving just two people in the game. If the second-highest bidder is at INR 1500 and the highest bidder is at INR 1600, the second-highest bidder must bid INR 1700 to prevent a sure shot loss of INR 1500. The uncertainty with the bidding seems more attractive than a certain loss. Very soon, they reach INR 1900 and INR 2000. Now what happens? Do they go on bidding? Yes, in reality, they keep on bidding to minimize the loss. But why do they bid past INR 2000? Because they are trapped by their need to minimize the loss, both psychologically and strategically. Their goal has now changed from winning the bid to minimizing the loss.

A client of mine, Samarth, was the head of sales for an industrial refrigeration company. They had pitched to a food processing plant and sent them a carefully drafted proposal. The plant came back with questions like "If we don't take this, what is the cost?", "If we don't take that what is the cost?" and tried to break the product into smaller sub-components and negotiate them individually. Why? Because negotiating sub-component individually will force Samarth to compromise on each. And each significant price compromise will force Samarth to compromise on features and quality as well. Samarth's goal was to provide the best possible solution as per the plant's specifications. He told the plant that he would not be negotiating each sub-component separately and politely walked out of the negotiation. Had he been needy for the deal or that his goal was just to get the client, Samarth would have compromised. A few weeks later, the plant called up Samarth and awarded them the contract.

If the goals that we set for us are not clearly defined, then oftentimes we become so invested to prove ourselves that we lose track of our objectives. If you are not working on behalf of your own goals, you are working on behalf of someone else's.

Lewis Carroll in his masterpiece 'Alice in Wonderful' illustrates the point with this short discussion between Alice and the Cheshire Cat.

Alice: "Would you tell me, please, which way I ought to go from here?"

The Cheshire Cat: "That depends a good deal on where you want to get to."

Alice: "I don't much care where."

The Cheshire Cat: "Then it doesn't much matter which way you go."

YOU NEED YOUR COUNTERPART TO SAVE FACE ALL THE TIME

A few years ago, we were once speaking to a small business for a coaching engagement. The business was into the hospitality industry running a business hotel in Durgapur. They were seeking to train their employees and had contacted multiple organizations who could deliver the training. We had a few rounds of discussions, but things weren't moving. The discussion dragged on for many weeks and somehow or the other the deal wasn't finalized. At the final stage, there were three organizations they had shortlisted but the company had not finalized any till then.

We tried to probe their HR Manager further asking her questions on why things weren't moving, but we got stalled. Was there some issue with us? Or, was it that the company did not need the coaching? What were the hidden factor that was stopping us? The company however remained tightlipped and kept skirting the issue. We couldn't crack them for the information. It was maddening to have a one-sided discussion with them, but tried to maintain our composure all the time.

So, we decided to reduce the number of man-hours involved in the discussion and cut down any more time spent. So, we called her up and said, "Ma'am, it seems that we are not able to get to a conclusion regarding the deal. We are sorry but we are unable to understand the reason behind the same. It feels like we are not in a mutually agreeable position to go ahead with the contract. However, we would love to work with you in future and are open to collaborate in any manner possible. Do let us know as and when any further services would be necessary for you and we can have our team take that forward."

Few months flew by and we had forgotten the incident. One day, we received a sudden call from the company's HR manager asking us if we can start the coaching engagement within the next few weeks. We were taken aback. We weren't expecting a call from them, leave alone, a direct request for starting the engagement.

"Hello, can you start the coaching engagement by end of May?" she asked

We held back our disbelief. "Hi, let me check with my team and get back to you," our office responded. Two days later, we called them up, "Hi, we can start the engagement, but most of our slots are booked till the end of May. However, we can give you slots from June. Would that be okay with you?"

"Yes that is good. Can you send me a proforma invoice?" she asked.

"We will share it on your email. However, we have to inform you that our costs have marginally increased due to logistical factors, so there would be an increase in the amount earlier quoted to you," we replied.

"How much?" she asked.

Keeping her on hold, we went through our calculations and then said, "by about 10%."

She paused for a few seconds mulling over the figure. "Done. Send me the invoice." The deal was sealed.

Few days into the training, we asked the HR manager what made them finalize the engagement and that too with us. We knew there were two more organizations also in the run for this contract. The reason she gave opened our eyes to a new dimension in negotiation.

She said, "We are really sorry that we couldn't finalize the deal earlier. There were some legal emergencies that we had to take care and we couldn't be explicit about it. We appreciate that you understood our difficulties. So, we called you up as soon as we were over with the emergencies. Actually you weren't the lowest bidder. But we wouldn't have given it to the others as they behaved quite rudely and wrote to the company Director when the discussions were stuck. We liked the fact that you were cognizant of our condition."

This was an Aha! moment for us. We later realized that what we had done out of courtesy was that we saved their face when things weren't turning out well.

Saving face means respecting the counterparts' dignity even when there is no deal. It is significant part of the negotiation process that the counterpart does not feel humiliated or lose their reputation. It is a big thing – as we say, your reputation as a negotiator always precedes you. Negotiations even when done on a professional level often have an element of personal involvement. The way a negotiation proceeds and ends often becomes a way to validate self-worth and build self-esteem. Unless the counterpart saves face, they will be reluctant to change their position or behavior or change their stance regarding the deal. If we try to humiliate them at any point in the negotiation process, they will be inclined to do things that may save their ego but destroy the value.

We weren't the lowest bidder, but we still got the engagement in this case. The HR manager came to us even if the transaction was costly for them.

Here are some phrases that can reduce tension and help your counterpart save face, when you know they may have said something that can hamper the negotiations.

- "Apparently, this can be interpreted in different ways..."
- "Possibly there are further reasons that we aren't aware of..."
- "Have a look at some of these information that you maybe did not have access to..."
- "I appreciate your inference, but have you thought about..."

CHAPTER SUMMARY

Being needy makes you vulnerable. Like predators instinctively look for prey, human beings can also smell neediness when they are around one. The only way to prevent getting taken for a ride during negotiation is to prevent your neediness from showing during the discussion. The only person who is okay to be needy is your counterpart.

Here are the key takeaways from the chapter:

- As you step into the world of negotiations, the first and the most important idea that you have to keep in mind is that you cannot become too needy for a deal. Neediness betrays your desire to close a deal at any cost, even if it puts you at risk. The moment

Neediness

you become needy, it starts showing in the interactions, either through actions or behavior. In a business negotiation, showing your neediness puts you at an immediate disadvantage. Why start with a losing mindset?

- Neediness can be exhibited in different ways, through handing out unnecessary concessions to close the deal, too much talking, pleading or through an expression of anger and frustration on how and what the counterpart is saying. Fear of failure and fear of rejection are the two most important barriers you have to cross before getting to the deal table. You need to be able to walk away from a deal that you don't like. However, wanting something is perfectly fine and you can guide your counterpart to what you want.

- If at any point in time, you feel too needy about a deal; take a step back, evaluate your options and figure out how to restructure yourself and frame your points in a way that makes your counterpart needy for the deal. If nothing works out or you feel squeezed to the extent of suffocation, quit the deal. It's like pulling a Band-Aid – do you want a slow painful release or one quick release?

- Not being needy also means that you need not strip the counterpart to their bare bones. There is nothing to prove in a negotiation if you know what you want out of the deal. Your counterpart is not your enemy - you are at the deal table because both you and your counterpart want something out of the deal. And since beating your counterpart, figuratively (and sometimes literally), is not your goal, let them save face. Do not embarrass them at the deal table, with their team or within your internal team or anywhere. You may often find that what is not negotiable today may become negotiable tomorrow and you want what your counterpart is offering.

BUILD THE BRIDGE

"Can you come to my office? Immediately. No excuses." It was 6:30 PM on a Saturday evening. The day was over and it was packing time. I had sent the last email for the day and was stuffing my laptop into the bag. There was a soft soothing breeze outside, just perfect to go out for a relaxing run after office – an impeccable way to wind-up the week. It had been a hectic 6-days, so I was enthusiastically looking for a stress-free evening. The call was not from my boss. Ayan Mukherjee called. Ayan was a good friend of mine. We grew up together. We knew each other from the time we were ten years old. He was now the Zonal Manager for Eastern India for a Consumer Health Products Company.

"How quickly can you come?" Ayan asked. Over the phone, it felt like there was an unnerving apprehension in his voice. It is not often that he gets so anxious.

I glanced at my watch, "Will be there in 45 minutes."

Ayan had grown up through a rough childhood. Life had thrown him a lot of challenges over time, but he had withstood most of the blows. He was a hardened guy, someone who dared to look at challenges in the eye and take decisions which others found difficult. Hearing an uneasy Ayan is something rare. And he didn't open up to people easily. Something was really pressing. This needed immediate intervention.

Forty-five minutes later, I entered his smoke-filled cabin. He had been on a smoking spree. It was difficult to breathe in there. The acrid smoke choked up the mood and prevented clear thoughts. I signaled to the office boy to turn up the air-conditioner and sat down on the sofa. For the next thirty minutes, Ayan stared out of the glass window puffing away cigarettes one after another. He started to say something then stopped. For third time he had tried to express himself. It was related to another member of his team Monalisa. The vibe was of someone who had got rattled pretty badly.

The only thing Ayan was scared of was emotions. Both his own, and that of others. He could stomp on seemingly impossible tasks you throw his way. He could logically wrap his mind around almost anything. The only thing that strained him was emotional people. He found it difficult, in fact too difficult to deal with emotions of others. Over a period of time and several recurring personal issues later, he had hardened his own emotions and his reaction to that of others. Whenever he was faced with emotionally charged situations, his opening reaction was to counter with logical answers. He drove straight to the point, what was bothering the person and tried to find out logical next steps.

If you have ever dealt with emotionally charged situations, you would know that this apparently rational approach is the worst problem-solving approach you can take. Many still fall into this trap. Painstakingly true especially for men, whose primary reaction is to analyze the circumstances, find out how to resolve the issue and get done with. Women, on the other hand, are naturally more inclined to hear out the person.

OUR CURRENT ACTIONS INFLUENCED BY PAST EXPERIENCES

How we respond to a situation depends on our past experiences. It is classical conditioning that if we repeatedly get rewarded for a particular behavior, we are more prone to repeat the same behavior under similar circumstances.

Take for example, Mukund, my colleague and his wife who were discussing where to go out for Sunday brunch. Mukund wanted to go for an exquisite upscale place preferably where they could relax, roll up their sleeves and have a good time. Mukund looked up online - browsing through listing sites filtering on the ratings, reviews and aesthetics of the restaurants. His wife took the laptop and started putting up the price filters. "This restaurant," she said pointing to the screen, "is too expensive. INR 500 for just a salad!" "Neither this one," she pointed to another one, "Look at the quantity that they serve for this sky-high price." Both Mukund and his wife were senior working professional and they could afford these restaurants as a one-off.

The difference was their upbringing. Mukund's family was comfortably secure. Though not from a very prolific background, he never had to complain. His childhood had never been demanding enough. His wife on the other hand, had been through exasperating times while growing up. She had observed her mother and father go through ups and downs, frantically trying to save every dime and bargaining hard for everyday items. Even though the situation had changed today, their current actions were still getting commandeered by their past experiences.

Same was with Ayan. Emotions didn't have a place in his professional life now. That was his way of going through troubles. He found it difficult to navigate sensitive circumstances. He got muddled wherever he had to confront emotionally charged problems. So, before I could understand Monalisa's issue, I had to sort out Ayan's state. I had to wait for the fog to clear before I could get on the road.

SLOW DOWN THE CAR

Negotiations in itself is chockfull of apprehensions. Parties come to the table with a pre-decided set of agenda and are engrossed in their own demands. Submerged in their own thoughts, they often fail to look at or understand what the counterpart is going through. Some negotiations start off on highly sensitive note, like an angry customer demanding for what's due, a deranged business partner eager to tear apart the other partner over issues he feels violated about, clients ripping through vendors over pricing or product quality, spouses dragging each other to court, departments within the same organization skeptical about the other's abilities, or students inadvertently rubbing their professors the wrong way. The counterpart is angry, aggressive, hurt or emotional about the outcome. And in all such cases, you, as a negotiator, have to understand that locking horns and engaging under emotion with the counterpart will lead to a spiraling mess. You have to methodically break down the barrier and make yourself more approachable. You have to show them that you are willing to appreciate their point of view. And if you are at fault, mend the relationship before it gets awry.

Passage of time has wonderful effects on our emotions. The more time it gets, the more its grip loosens. It's like taking the pressure cooker off from the gas-top. Even if the fire is turned off, the steam still takes time to dissipate.

Ayan was swept up with a flurry of emotions. He needed time to clear the haze in his mind and before he could absorb what I was saying.

"Why don't you have a glass of water and sit here! It seems that you are going through very intense feelings now. Would it be okay to share what had happened?" I asked and handed him a glass of water.

Ayan continued to stare out through the tinted window glass into the gloomy night sky.

"It seems that this is an immensely difficult situation for you."

Ayan took a sip and sat down on the chair. His face still tensed and shoulders taut. "Monalisa spoke to me today afternoon. She wants to quit."

"She wants to quit?", I echoed and leaned forward towards Ayan.

"Yes, she wants to quit. She is a key resource in my team and handles all the critical activities."

"Did she tell you why?", I asked.

Ayan gawked at me and slumped in the chair, "The moment I heard her I reacted vigorously and shouted back at her. I used the choicest of words, but then, there was a lot going on in my mind. I was so upset that I probably didn't let her speak. How can she, after being so many years in the company, be so impulsive!"

"Hmm...," I said.

"After that, Monalisa rushed out of the office. I shouldn't have reacted in that way. She must have her reasons." Ayan was realizing that he should have not reacted.

Another snail-pace thirty minutes into the discussion, Ayan started opening up more about what happened that day. Emotions are like onions. Layers and layers are wrapping the core. You have to keep peeling them till you get to the essence. Once Ayan had been taken care of, it was time to come to the core concern – understanding Monalisa.

Monalisa was with the company for more than 8 years. She had grown through the ranks and had been a strong foundation for the team. Monalisa was an exceptionally respected member of the team. She had seen the company go through bitter hardships, devastating setbacks and adventurous good times – always being with the company and standing rock-solid beside Ayan wherever it was necessary. She had exceptional work ethics, completed her work on time, had introduced several noteworthy processes and products and had been honored as top performer more than a few times.

However, off late, she had been distant from Ayan and the team.

She had restricted herself to her cubicle, not interacting with the team except for work. Her quality of work continued to be on par, but she was reserved. Ayan had noticed the change but overlooked it. He thought this might go away with time. But it had come back to haunt him now. There were two fallbacks if Monalisa resigned. One, it would be difficult to find someone of her caliber who can shoulder the critical activities. The learning curve would be awfully steep and the new joinee would take weeks to pick up. Secondly, this would be a psychological setback for the entire team. She was revered by the team.

"Ayan, listen," I said, "What you have to do is to not react but to respond to the situation. Both you and Monalisa are going through some sort of turmoil and it is better to address the situation upfront. Get on a call with her and I will tell you how to go about it. Pick up the phone and apologize to her."

Ayan cut me out. "Why should I apologize? It was not my fault. I did not start this goddamn thing."

BUILDING THE BRIDGE

I am closely associated with many organizations for their training requirements. We are called from time to time to take certain training sessions for their employees. Participants in training sessions are often withdrawn initially. They are skeptical of the day ahead of them. Think of it like a car with an old diesel engine. It takes multiple tries and continuous revving of the keys to warm up the engine before it starts. While participants are willing to learn new ideas, they aren't accepting enough to opening up in front of a third party. The first fifteen minutes of any training session is a negotiation with the participants. Not a direct negotiation, but one where I have to negotiate with their reservations and establish myself as someone they would want to hear from.

The most prevalent method is where the coach puts up a slide and read out a list of achievements and credentials that he has, covering academic credentials, work achievements, positions held and so on and so forth. This, in my view, is a pure waste of energy. Never have I ever seen in my career that credentials and past achievements cause an audience to become engaged. Listening to a speaker or a coach who puffs up his own self-worth is not an enjoyable experience. Paradoxically it's difficult to take someone like this seriously. No one likes to hear someone beating his own drums. But session after session, speakers and trainers keep on doing this. One, this is easier. It is minimal investment of energy on behalf of the trainer. And secondly, it gives a false sense of control. Establishing that one is superior to the audience in some aspects is a sure shot of disengaging the audience. Credentials are important but not as a way to build connections with the audience.

The alternate method is one that most don't take. But it is the most effective one. An audience would engage with you only if you can establish a rapport with them quickly enough. There are two shortcut approaches to building rapport - to start either with humor or an apology.

Let's break it down. A humor is an ice-breaker. A speaker who uses humor comes across as more likeable and open. If you can get someone to laugh you can build an instant connection. John Cleese, an English actor and comedian has said, "He who laughs most, learns best."

In his 2009 TED Talk, Bill Gates was speaking on the topic of malaria, one of the deadliest disease that affects humans. Malaria has several serious complications and an important cause of stillbirths, infant mortality, abortion, and low birth weight. In this speech, he quipped, "because the disease is only in the poorer countries, it doesn't get much investment. For example, there's more money put into baldness drugs than are put into malaria. Now, baldness, it's a terrible thing. And rich men are afflicted. And so that's why that priority has been set. "

That is a brilliant example of using humor to drive home a point.

Everyone likes to laugh – it is a positive feeling. An audience will love you if you can make them laugh. And if you can convey a message through humor, they will swoon over you. What humor does is provide an escape from the mundane and helps the audience forget, albeit temporarily, their pains and troubles. Humor used correctly is a recruiter to get people on your side. Making something fun will make people likely to come along with you and enjoy the journey together.

A speaker who uses humor well comes across as more human, more likeable. This puts an audience at ease and makes people more receptive to your ideas. As British comedian John Cleese has said, "If I can get you to laugh with me, you like me better, which makes you more open to my ideas."

Another opening technique that I use is an apology.

APOLOGIES, MY BAD!

What? You say! Did you read properly? Yes, it is to start with an apology. A great technique used by master negotiators is showing that they are somewhat not up to the mark compared to their adversaries. This technique works excellently for counterparts who are superior to you or doubtful about you. This also works for aggressive or emotional counterparts, people who have grievances against you or those who harbor resentment. Even for counterparts who do not fit these categories, an apology never backfires. This concept goes against the prevalent concept that negotiators must always establish themselves as superior and that is why this concept is difficult to grasp right away. But an apology can take you places you never imagined, even if it is your counterpart who has erred on their part.

In some sessions that I take, participants are older to me by age. They have more expertise in their field of work – some would have worked in the domain for 20 to 30 years and have immense subject matter expertise in their respective domains. They would have spent their life mastering skills specific to their jobs. Getting them to appreciate that an outsider can bring a fresh perspective is a challenge. Getting the audience to open up and listen to what I present without dismissing them right away is a challenge. How do I establish a rapport with the audience and get them to also appreciate my points of view?

I start with an apology.

"I do not have the expertise or the know-how that you have in your fields. You are masters of your own domains. What I am here for is to present some facts to you and you can decide for yourself if these are helpful in your work."

See how this sentence is crafted.

It starts with an apology that my domain knowledge is not comparable to their years of expertise. What this does is to bring out into open any possible negative sentiment the audience might have and lay them bare on the table. Any possible allegation the audience may have is provoked out. Once I have accepted that I am in no way superior to the audience, they become more receptive to what I have to say.

In the same sentence, I acknowledge their superior skills. A big massage to their ego. Everybody loves an ego massage. Then I invite them to keep their minds open and listen to my propositions without having to accept them. The audience has nothing to lose here. I am not forcing them to accept my viewpoints. I am requesting them to listen. What harm can 'listening' do? Since this is non-committal on part of the audience, they have nothing to lose. This is similar to the "Trial Close", where products and services are offered on a trial basis and you can buy the full version or the premium version if you like the product.

DIFFUSE THE NEGATIVE

A colleague of mine, Sonia used the apology technique to get out of a tricky situation and make an ally out of her boss. She was heading the unit for a critical client project that needed to get delivered by a deadline.

However, the estimate showed that the project will not get delivered on time. The client was a very influential one with senior connections. One call from him to the head of the organization and it would become a spiraling mess. If not pacified in time, people could be sacked.

Apologies can be used in different ways in a negotiation. Take for example a scenario that you would have gone through often but not noticed. I would like you to appreciate the fact that even though you have heard it multiple times, it has the same desired effect every time you hear it. Look at how trained call center personnel deals with angry customers – "I am sorry sir that you got impacted due to the breakdown in our services." Or how a friend warns you that he is going to say something really bad – "I do not mean to make you feel bad, but…"

An apology gets the sting out from the accusations and disarms the opponent. After all, if someone has owned up, how further can you press charges! An apology can create value on its own. Negotiators must look at intangible interests along with tangible results. There are umpteen cases where parties value an apology for the emotional trauma much more than receiving a tangible outcome. An apology can be used to solidify intangibles and resolve conflicts in a way that tangibles alone can't. Apology serves a basic human need and prevents conflicts from escalating. An apology can heal emotional trauma and allow adversaries to move on.

In negotiations, an apology may be unavoidable. In many cases, to get to where you want, you'll do or say something that rubs the other person the wrong way and hurts your counterpart. Even if the harm you cause is unintentional, you will have to rebuild the bridge and repair the connection to have the negotiations continue.

With this knowledge about apologies, about 2 days before the deadline, Sonia called up her boss.

"I am sorry. You may feel that I am incompetent and cannot live up to the organizational standards," she said.

There was a long silence on the line.

Sonia paused and then continued "I have failed to keep up with the commitment that was given to the client. The project will not get delivered on time. I feel terrible about this and I am ready to take up the responsibility for the failure. I am sorry to put you in such a demanding situation." She paused again, letting the sentence sink in.

"I am sorry" is the hardest phrase to say but the most effective when dealing with people in power. The negative had to be pulled up front and diffused. If there is one thing that you can learn about human behavior now is that when you own up to mistakes, you diffuse the accusations that would have anyways surfaced.

"You have known all through that the deadline is coming up," his boss said, his voice revealed his irritation.

"It is entirely my mistake. I am willing to take full responsibility for failure. We have been working hard on this project, but some last moment glitches came up in the underlying technology. Our team is putting in extra efforts to debug and get the project back on track. This is something that we have not anticipated and we got derailed," she gave a brief pause. Then she added, "If I have your support, may I speak to the client directly and explain the position to him."

Oh, what a reverse! There you go. She just made her boss an ally in this negotiation. Taking up responsibility for the debacle, Sonia pitched her boss for his support. She did not ask her boss to talk to the client – she quickly absolves her boss and requests him to back her.

"This is not what I expected from an experienced team lead as you." His boss sighed. "Take me on the call with the client. Let us see how we can work this out with the client."

Sonia's objective was achieved. With her boss on her side, he had a better chance of pacifying the client.

To ensure that your apology is sincere, have one or more of the following components in your apology:

1. Issue an apology – "I am sorry."
2. Follow this up with an expression of regret – "I feel terrible about …"
3. Put in a bit of self-blame – "I am solely responsible for this disaster."
4. Ask for forgiveness – "Kindly accept my apology."
5. Offer your adversary an escape route – "I am ready to take up the responsibility of this failure."
6. Promise future action – "I will find a way out."
7. Offer an explanation - "I failed to deliver because…"
8. Recruit your adversary on your side – "If I have your support…"

Try this the next time you are have messed up and see the amazing results it gives.

There may be cases where an apology will fall on deaf ears. An apology may fail to come to the desired outcome. This is more attributable to the delivery rather than the concept of apology. If delivered sincerely and with the right intent, your apology will achieve its anticipated objective. However, if your adversary feels that the apology is insincere, he will be unlikely to absolve you.

BE LESS PERFECT

Apologies are one way of showing that you are not perfect. Showing a vulnerable side makes the communication more humane and strikes an immediate chord with the adversary. Have you ever felt uncomfortable being in front of someone who made you feel inferior? Everybody has. Have you felt awkward when someone made you feel mediocre? I think so. How do you feel when you interact with someone who is perfect in dressing and speaking? Uneasy, right? So, if you come up as perfect, you are actually making the counterpart feel uneasy.

The only person who is okay to feel superior is your counterpart. You want the deal to happen in your favor. You don't bother what the counterpart feels of himself. Even, if that requires you to influence your counterpart to feel superior.

Bishal from our sales team does this perfectly. Whenever, he meets a customer for the first time, he pretends that his pen has run out of ink. And then goes to borrow a pen from the customer. This does two things. One, he ensures that the customer feels a bit superior to Bishal and this increases the chance of a favorable discussion. And Secondly, Bishal employs the Ben Franklin Effect, which says that if someone does you a favor that person starts liking you more. More on this effect in the later chapters.

Next time, try to be a bit off your mark. Pretend you forgot your pen or notebook, or you slipped the pen from your hand and picked it up, or fumble in finding out the file from your laptop folder.

"I am sorry; I do not seem to be able to find the document file in my laptop drive. So sorry to keep you waiting."

In most cases, the response will be empathetic, "It is okay. Take your time."

This point is hard for people to accept. I get questions like "Wouldn't that be unprofessional?" or "Won't they tell me to come prepared next time?" No, they wouldn't, unless you are taking up too much of their time. They wouldn't even notice it. On the contrary, they will offer you something in return like a piece of paper or pen or, even more valuable, their time.

Practice it a few times and see the charm.

That fateful evening, I coached Ayan and convinced him to get on the phone with Monalisa. He started, "I am sorry for reacting that way. I feel bad about overreacting without hearing your side of the story." He paused for three seconds allowing Monalisa to absorb these words and come to terms with the situation.

"You are a valuable member of the team and we do not want to lose you. If you can help me understand the situation, we may be able to work out a solution."

Another few seconds passed before Monalisa responded, "Ok"

That was the sign that she had numbed down a bit and willing to come down for a discussion with Ayan.

CHAPTER SUMMARY

Get your counterpart comfortable enough to start the discussions. Most approach negotiations with the optimism to share information, develop a working relationship and be treated fairly by counterparts. But once the discussion begins and as each side starts presenting their views, we start viewing the other side's behavior with suspicion. If parties are skeptical of each other, then effective negotiations break down and lead to bruised egos and bad names. Effective negotiations can take place only when there is mutual trust between parties.

Meeting new negotiators or coming to the table for the first time also requires building the relationship bridge. It is about communicating with your counterpart that you can be trusted and respected. It requires establishing the right connections to start the discussions.

Here are the key takeaways from this chapter:

- Our current actions are shaped by our past experiences. Whenever your counterpart is skeptical or distrusting from the beginning of the negotiation, there would have been precedence where they might have been treated wrongly or taken for a ride. The key here is to breakdown those initial barriers to communication and get the ball rolling.

- Slow down. If your counterpart is flushed with emotions, it is important to slow down the discussions. The more time passes, the easier it becomes for emotions to dissipate. Going too fast gives off a negative vibe to your counterpart that you are not willing to hear them. Interrupt whenever someone is going fast in the negotiation, whether it is you or your counterpart.

- Negotiations are inherently stressful. Whether it is a first-time negotiation or repeated negotiation with the same counterpart. Either side comes to the table with certain expectations and wants. And in such situations, there is bound to be passionate reactions to demands. Use humor to establish an instant connection. Humor breaks down barriers, induces positive emotions, triggers positive communications and eases the conversation. Using humor appropriately can untangle negative sentiments between counterparts and build quick rapport.

- Apologies, on the other hand, breaks down the negative dynamics. When your opponent is critical of your competencies or holds you in a negative light, go straight at the negativity with an apology. If the counterparts feel they have been treated wrongly or taken for granted (even if that was not factually right and you believe otherwise), start with an apology. If an apology is sincere, your opponent will accept it and go past confrontational undercurrents.

- "I am sorry" is the most difficult but most effective phrase to cut through all the negativity and get to the core of the issue. It opens up the suppressed emotions and gets them to the surface. If you own up before your counterpart gets the opportunity to accuse you of something, the negative effect diminishes greatly.

- No one likes a glib talking salesperson. Show that you are not perfect. It humanizes the interaction and lets the counterpart lower their guards. Don't do something overly bad like a torn shirt, but smaller inconsequential things.

VOID YOUR MIND

Ayan asked Monalisa to meet him the following Monday.

"What do I do next?" Ayan asked me.

"Nothing," I quipped.

"Earnestly asking. What do I do?" Ayan pressed.

"Nothing. Just listen to her."

Listening is one of the least used and most magical of skills in any negotiation. Most people balk at the notion of learning listening skills, especially since they have been using this their entire life. We think that our listening skills are above average. Truth is that all of us can improve our listening skills. You would be amazed at how skilled negotiators use listening skills to resolve conflicts. If it wasn't that important, there wouldn't be a chapter on it. I learned it the hard way.

It was one of my first sales interactions. We were selling courses for the academy. Leads used to come in from online listings and web forms that prospects would fill up enquiring about the courses. The sales team's role was to call the lead, follow-up with hot leads and get them to walk-in to the academy. This process was arduous and demanding, requiring us to go through piles of cold leads, evaluate each one of them, shortlist the good ones and finally pursue those that fit our criteria. It was quite a task and so every walk-in lead was 'high priority' for us. I was learning tricks of the trade and finally got a lead who wanted to come down to our office for more details about the courses.

It was D-Day. I dressed up in my best blue shirt together with a matching tie and polished shoes. We were all set for the lead. The earlier night had gone into preparing the sales pitch, revising how to pitch, what to say and how to present the features and benefits of the course. The entire pitch was memorized by heart and I could recite it even in the middle of the night. A lot of efforts had gone into preparing the pitch, accumulating collaterals, testimonials, speaking to mentors and experts in sales.

The lead walked in and we welcomed him to my cubicle.

"Good morning! Thank you so much for coming."

"Good morning!" he replied, "Could you tell me the admission process and the fees for the course?"

"Sure! We will assist you." I jumped into my well-rehearsed pitch. It was a superb feeling knowing exactly what, when and how to say. I went on for fifteen minutes explaining in picturesque detail what the course entails, how it will help him and benefits that would support his learning goals. Every nod from him pumped me up enthusiastically, like pouring gas on the fire.

When the pitch was over, I wrote down the fees on a piece of paper and handed it over to him.

He looked hard at the number and then at me. My heart skipped a beat. His eyes twitched and eyebrows furrowed as if there was something amiss. "Hmm, this is ..." I cut him off mid-sentence.

"No worries, I can give you a 40% discount on the course." I blurted.

A tight little smile formed on the corner of his lips and his eyes twinkled. Then, he broke into a wide smile, "Well, this is something I have been looking for. It's well within my budget but I would gladly accept a 40% discount."

I made a rookie mistake. I was too full in my head. I read too much into his expressions. No one had taught me to listen.

FIRST THINGS FIRST

Before getting into listening (which will get covered in the next chapter), we will deal with the prerequisites for listening in this chapter. How to we prepare ourselves to listen? What are the key imperatives that a negotiator must keep in mind before starting the negotiation?

Listening is hard. It requires a lot of discipline. It cannot be mastered overnight. Why? Because, most people listen with the intent to reply. However, that will not serve the purpose for a negotiator. A negotiator must be ready to listen all in and with no intent of replying. Just being there like a sponge to soak up any and everything that is thrown at him. Most negotiators make the mistake of speaking too soon and too much. This is deep-rooted culturally. All those negotiation movies that you see have the protagonist use their gift of the gab to convince the counterpart and subduing them into submission. But what happens in real life is far different from these fancy movies. A good negotiator spends a lot of time listening, understanding the counterpart's views and absorbing as much as possible from the interactions.

What hinders effective listening?

Firstly, many feel that negotiation is active persuasion and that requires overpowering their counterpart with logic and words. These people see *listening* as passive and *talking* as active participation in the negotiation. They forget that people cannot be persuaded until you know what drives them. What is your gut feeling when you see a smooth-talking sales guy? Uncomfortable, right? There is a term for such sales scenarios. It's called spray and pray. The salesperson vomits volumes of information and prays that the customer will find something interesting or something that fits their needs.

Secondly, most people prepare negotiations with a view of questions and counter questions. What should be their response to objections and questions thrown by the counterpart? How they should frame their next set of arguments? They spend their listening time thinking and framing their responses.

Thirdly, what we hear and what we perceive is different. Think of it as light falling on a red velvet cloth. The cloth looks red because it reflects the red spectrum and absorbs the other wavelengths. Most of us listen in a similar way – we are selective in letting one spectrum of information being processed and the others are ignored. We are selective in what we listen, we hear what we want to hear and ignore the rest. This is cognitive bias - to interpret consistent to our perception of the reality rather than the reality itself. We as individuals create our own "subjective reality" from the perception of the input. And this construction of the reality dictates how we act and behave.

VOIDING THE MIND

To get into listening mode, we have to void our mind. Voiding the mind requires removal of all excitements, expectations and biases from the mind, so that it is ready to receive new information from the counterpart. It is like a vacuum that will soak in anything and everything the counterpart says without distorting it in any fashion. It is like a blank chart paper waiting to be written on. It is like the clear distilled water which does not have a tint of its own.

Voiding the mind requires a significant behavioral change – one where we control the urge to color the incoming information. We hear the information as it is without tainting it with our interpretation. We neither agree nor disagree to what is being said. We accept the counterpart's words for what it is, nothing more nothing less. We absorb the words being said, how it is being said, and what body language is being used. We force ourselves to listen without the intent of replying. This change of behavior takes time but it is worth the effort.

Voiding entails getting rid of all expectations and assumptions. Very hard for most, but this is the first step.

SLIPPERY SLOPE OF EXPECTATIONS

Saugat, a friend of mine, runs an animation and design firm. He is a superb animator and does work for several production houses across India, including multiple television and film productions. The quality of his work was at par with the best in the market and he had a reputation of on-time delivery. Up to this time, he had been working with mostly mid-size productions houses, though he had done few stints with the larger houses as well. Few months back, he received an offer from one of the largest production houses in India. Here is an account of how the discussion went.

"Hi Saugat, we are looking for an experienced animation firm for an upcoming content. We have been following your work closely for the past few months and we are impressed by the quality and freshness in your deliverables. We would love to work with you."

Saugat was exhilarated. It was a dream come true. This was one of the most sought after production houses and he was ecstatic at the offer. To this day, he had only dreamt of tying up with them. And that day, it felt so real. He could smell success. "Sure. We can take up work for your content."

"We are looking at outsourcing to your firm about 20000 seconds per month and will be increased further depending on the quality of work in the few next months."

Typically, Saugat's firm worked with small to mid-sized production houses which outsourced about 1000 to 2000 seconds per month. 20000 seconds was like a striking a gold mine. He was unable to stop his excitement. He had finally made it to the scene. At standard per-unit cost of about INR 300 per second, it translated to INR 60 Lakhs – an eye-popping number.

The representative of the production house continued, "As this is bulk outsourcing, we are looking for a discount on standard rates."

Even with some discount, that translated to a huge number and could take his firm to the A-league. Saugat called them back ready with calculations: "We can work out about 15% discount for you."

Production House: "We are looking at a 30% discount. We will not involve any other firm and outsource the entire project to you."

Saugat did some calculations in his mind. A 30% discount still translated to INR 42 Lakhs project, a bit less than INR 60 Lakhs but a lot more than what he was making now. This INR 42 Lakhs would cover all his costs and still leave him a substantial profit.

"Yes, we will go ahead with the project. When do we start?"

Production House: "We will call you back with the details. We are finalizing INR 210 per second as the rate."

The production house came back after 2 weeks.

"Hi, Saugat. How are you? We have some good and bad news for you. The bad news is that we miscalculated their project size and it would be a total of around 8000 seconds per month. We are sorry! Some of our existing vendors are also working and we have to maintain relationships with all vendors. So, we are dividing the project amongst all. The good news is that despite all of this, we are very eager to work with you and so, we fought for you with our senior management and got you a piece of the project. That would come at about 1500 seconds for you."

With this, they also hinted that they would be disappointed if Saugat said "no" to the project. They were very interested to work with the expertise that his firm brings to the table.

Now look at what has happened. This is a classic case of not voiding the mind during the negotiation. The production house created so compelling a positive expectation that Saugat could not keep his mind voided during the negotiation. He was swept off the floor with massive numbers and a rosy future. This expectation-pumping trick has been applied for ages and people still fall for them. It triggers a strong positive excitement which clouds rational thinking. And positive expectations feel good. It is progressive and futuristic. It is what has been preached as a growth mindset by coaches and trainers across the globe. Think positive. And it is this mindset what some of these large companies exploit.

How do you deal with such situations? Don't let big numbers affect your judgement. Easier said than done; and requires a lot of self-discipline and meticulous focus to maintain an expectation-less state. There are different ways to deal with the situation. Take the high number thrown at you as just a number. It isn't finalized. It isn't written down in black and white. What you can do is outline a staggered pricing depending on the quantity of work. Or, do background research on the counterpart and whether they have the capacity to offer such large numbers. Do some fact-finding. Have they ever offered business of this extent? What is their market reputation? A bit of research will go a long way.

On the other extreme are negative expectations, where you do not expect an outcome from the discussion. This is equally bad. Negative expectations can take the form of not trying, quitting the negotiations even before it has reached a conclusion, or giving up at the outset.

I once almost lost a deal because of negative expectation. Remember the incident at the beginning of this chapter. Parallel to this discussion,

I was also following up with other leads who had visited our office and who were yet to make a decision. One particular lead had said that the pricing was on the higher side even with a discount and would not be looking at enrolling anytime soon. I had struck off the lead from my follow-up diary. Our asking price was higher than what she could afford. About a few weeks later, the lead called up and said she had managed to accumulate the course fees and was willing to register. She came down and registered the very next day.

It was one fortunate incident, but we couldn't leave this to chance anymore. Post this incident, we instituted a process to keep in touch with all leads (up to a certain time threshold) by sending them regular communications and materials about new developments in the business. That way, if situations change, we would be there in their mind space.

THE TRAP YOU LAY FOR YOURSELF

We were conducting interviews to recruit a subject matter expert for one of our departments. We have been looking for a senior resource to head the department for quite some time. Someone who had a good number of years of experience in this field and would be able to deliver on some of the key work we were doing.

After shuffling through multiple resumes, we found a candidate, Seema Dev, who could fit the role. Seema had 12 years of experience in a similar organization working with teams and had shown a lot of eagerness to deliver on our projects. She had worked in her earlier organization for a long time, showed a commitment towards organizational goals, was not finicky to change companies quickly and who would be with us in the journey. Her skills in the field was up to par and demonstrated an eagerness to learn more along the way.

Everyone in the team liked her and she got hired. About a month into the organization, we started receiving feedback about her inability to handle questions. Whenever someone asked her about work or her projects, she got sensitive and snapped. Seema quit her job the following week. What we later found out was that she could not stand being queried by others. She felt violated when someone quizzed her or put up casual requests with her.

A bigger sin than expectations is assumptions. We had assumed that someone with 10+ years of experience working with teams would have this primary skillset. We were wrong. Assumptions had clouded our judgement to put to test all aspects before hiring. By the time she quit, we had rejected all other candidates and had to start over again. The basic premise of avoiding assumptions could have saved us months of work.

Hypothesis lead, assumptions trap. Having a hypothesis about how the negotiation is going to play out can give a direction, provided that the hypothesis keeps changing as and when new information comes out. Assumptions are traps that you lay for yourself and this becomes a self-fulfilling prophecy. Your views of the world can obscure your judgement about how the negotiations can proceed.

Assumptions come in different forms. If you are negotiating to sell something, your assumptions can be:

- "He won't be able to afford the service."
- "Competition will kill us."
- "She doesn't have enough cash to fund the down payment."
- "He won't be taking our service anymore after the last mess we created."
- "I'm sure we're not the low bidder."
- "We don't have the capability to serve their massive requirements."

Think of the following example. Aisha is a shy girl who loved to read books. She had consistently topped her classes in school and college. Her teachers appreciated her tenacity to learn and improve her skills.

Void your Mind

Sunny on the other hand did not read much. He had a knack for playing football and used to spend lots of time on the playground or gossiping with friends. He barely scraped through exams. One of them grew up to be a librarian and the other took up a career in sales. Now answer the following question with the first thing that comes to your mind: Who is the librarian and who is in sales?

USING ASSUMPTIONS TO YOUR ADVANTAGE

Whoever assumes loses the deal. Master negotiators often seed the counterparts mind with assumptions to win the negotiation. I remember this one time I sold to a lead using assumptions to my advantage. He had come in asking for a course. He looked quite sophisticated and posh. Someone who would be willing to spend on a good course. When he was going through the course details, he pointed to one course and asked, "How much will this cost me to take up?" I replied, "this one is expensive," then pointed to another course in the list, "instead, you can go for this one."

Expensive to him meant quite a lot of money. It is a relative term meaning different for different people. Our courses were competitively priced compared to the market. When I finally gave him the actual figure, he felt relieved that it was within budget and made the payment immediately.

Another way to negotiate a sale using assumption to your advantage is to use the assumptive selling or presumptive closing technique. I couldn't be happier than to see a member of my team use this technique to close a deal.

Riyaz was a senior in the team in charge of this deal. He had been negotiating for us for more than 4 years now. He was an expert in fact finding and thoroughly prepared for every deal. He knew for one that any and all assumptions on his part can backfire. Based on available details, he found out about the lead's background, what were his obvious pain points, how the deal can help him and what objections can possibly come up.

One thing to note is that research and assumptions are not the same. Research is deepening your facts about the counterpart, assumptions are your inferences or expectations.

There was this lead, Alex Roy, who was working for a real estate firm. He had 8 years of experience in the construction industry on designing layout and plans for new projects for the firm. He was extremely adept at that with significant knowledge of market standards, what buyers for his industry valued, and how he could help his firm deliver amazing living spaces out of seemingly small areas. He was looking to upgrade himself and had found out about us from the internet.

Alex's pain point was that he had got stuck in his role because he hadn't upgraded himself with the newer technological tools. He was looking for a flexible training session preferably over the weekend to upskill himself. There can be different ways to research clients. One, for sure, is to ask the lead directly.

After the initial small talk, Riyaz started, "Could you please elaborate on your requirements?"

See! Riyaz did not say, "You want to upgrade yourself, right?" or worse still, "Are you looking to learn this tool for applying for a promotion?" That would be an outright assumption. He instead wanted to hear it from the lead.

Alex: "I have been in the construction industry for my entire career working on creating computer aided design plans. I joined my existing company when I was a fresher and have, since then, picked up skills and techniques to help me deliver in my work area. I am confident now that whatever be the design, I can design a plan according to the needs of the clients. But I am seeing that some new design tools are coming up in the market which makes it easier to create these plans. If I know these advanced tools, I can prepare myself to ask for a raise or switch jobs out of the city."

Riyaz listened to the lead and continued asking him more questions. Riyaz, then, proceeded to outline our offering and how it fits his requirement. After some more questions, when Riyaz was clear that most doubts were addressed, he paused and looked at the lead.

"We have a few open slots for the weekend. When should I schedule your classes – Weekend morning or afternoon?"

That is called the assumptive close where a part of the decision making process is bypassed on behalf of the counterpart. Usually, if you look at any sales, there are at least two decisions to be made by the prospect – the decision whether to buy or not; and the decision on how to take the delivery or how to implement. Decision making requires a lot of mental space. And that is taxing. This technique gives the counterpart one less decision to worry about – the decision whether to buy or not. This decision is removed from the table and his attention to the easier decision on delivery or implementation. The salesperson assumes that the counterpart has already agreed to the offerings and goes straight for closure by saying something like, 'When should we get begin implementation?' Other examples are:

- "When can we start the pilot project – tomorrow or day after?"
- "What delivery date would suit you?"
- "Which of these (package, tier, bundle, course, options) are you going with?"
- "Can you share these information (name, number, any other information) and I'll get the paperwork ready now."

This technique works amazingly if you have followed through the listening process, asked the right questions to the counterpart and cleared his objections from the discussion. Use this the next time and see the results.

BUILDING NEED WITH LESS TALKING

Remember a few chapters back we had discussed about Need versus Want. The concept applies here too. People feel the need to be heard. They want to resonate with someone, share what they feel and connect. Negotiations happen because two or more parties want to reach an outcome. One thing that works wonder for negotiation is to use the first half of face to face time for listening. Listening extracts information and gets your counterpart to reveal portions of their story which you can use to build their own need.

Take the earlier case of Riyaz. Being a trained sales negotiator, he started by asking questions to Alex to get him to open up. He had some hypothesis and was validating the hypothesis by listening. The more the person talks the more the person reveals information about himself or his needs.

Good salespeople know that you just need to convince the client regarding one or two aspects of the deal. You don't need the client to want all the product features. Just one or two most critical needs if addressed correctly can be used to close the deal. To know which one or two aspects the client needs, you have to void your mind and keep aside all expectations and assumptions. This is brilliantly outlined in this famous illustrative story showing how a salesperson built a need by voiding his mind.

A real estate agent takes a couple to see a home for sale. It is an old pre-owned building that would require a lot of fixing to get it back into shape. Usually for real-estate sales, buyers look for age of the property, condition of the flat, locations, markets nearby, distance to office, pricing, family size, space for parking vehicles and the like. But being an experienced negotiator, the agent had voided his mind and was eagerly waiting to absorb information as they come from the buyers.

Void your Mind

As they enter the building, the couple notices a beautiful Gulmohar tree across the road.

The agent asks the couple, "What do you think about the house?"

The wife says, "Rohan, look at the beautiful Gulmohar tree. Ever since I was a girl, I always wanted to have a house with a Gulmohar tree in front."

Rohan: "Keep quiet and let us see the house first."

The agent is a seasoned salesperson. He takes them through the front door saying, "There are some changes that need to be done, but you can see this beautiful Gulmohar tree right from the living room, Mrs. Singh."

The master bedroom extended into the verandah overlooking the front of the house. As the agent takes them into the bedroom, Rohan says, "The false ceiling needs to be replaced."

The agent says, "And from here, you can see the beautiful Gulmohar tree, Mrs. Singh."

They then move to the rooftop. Rohan says, "The roof is dilapidated. This needs to be repaired and painted." The agent says, "And, you can see the beautiful Gulmohar tree even from the rooftop, Mrs. Singh."

As they are walking down the stairs, the agent says, "See, the beautiful Gulmohar tree is even visible from staircase windows, Mrs. Singh."

The agent shows the kitchen. Rohan: "The plumbing is leaking; these need to be replaced."

Agent says, "And while cooking, you can see the beautiful Gulmohar tree from here, Mrs. Singh."

You get the idea. At the end of the tour, the agent looks at Mrs. Singh and asks "Don't you like the house?"

Buying a house is far beyond a logical decision. It is more of a gut-feeling, an intuitive and feel-good decision that drives the sale. As agents know, wives have more influence on such decisions. He had pressed the right buttons.

Mrs. Singh, "Rohan, I do love the Gulmohar tree. It is something that our daughter will also like. You can negotiate on the rest, but I really like this place."

And eventually, they buy this place.

What is your client's Gulmohar tree? What is that one thing they cannot live without? What is one thing that they really love about your product or service? Finding out your client's Gulmohar tree requires you to discard your assumptions as to what will benefit your clients. Once you find the Gulmohar tree, build your client's need around that.

Many salespeople go over the top talking, talking and talking without bothering to ask the right questions! To build a need in the client's mind, we must listen to everything that they say. Ask more questions about their requirements, if needed. Once you have found the hot button, keep on pressing it till the deal is closed.

CHAPTER SUMMARY

Negotiations, by nature, are stressful. There will be things at stake and you would want to get the best out of that discussion. So, it goes without saying that a lot of thoughts will start clouding your mind. The key to starting the negotiation discussion is to remove expectations and assumptions from the equation. Voiding the mind takes time and effort – it won't come in a day.

Here are the key takeaways from this chapter:
- The first step to listening is to void the mind. Voiding entails that there are no expectations or assumptions in place before going into the negotiation. It is as if you have emptied all contents of the mind and are just waiting for it to receive new information,

Void your Mind 63

new ideas, or anything that comes.

- Expectations are obsessions with the possible outcome of the negotiation. It clouds your judgement and prevents you from being in the present. If your expectations run wild, the counterpart can easily sway you to make concessions or concede to their demands.

- Expectations can be positive or negative. Positive expectations entail beautiful rosy pictures of the outcome. It entices you to think big about the future sacrificing value in the present. While not all think-big are bad, this strategy can be employed by your counterpart to drive down prices or force you into making concessions. Negative expectations entail giving up on the negotiation. Both are equally harmful.

- A negotiator's worst enemy is the assumptions of the negotiation circumstances. These are conditional responses to certain stimuli, visual or otherwise, and prevent us from investigating in detail about the situation. The human mind is prone to conclude quickly based on an impartial understanding of the situation. In that case, you will often act immaturely and harm the negotiations.

- The more you listen the more you weapon you have to build your counterpart's needs.

ACTIVE LISTENING

On Monday morning at 9 AM, Ayan walked into his office with me by his side. That day would define the path his company will take for the next one year.

Ayan had restless nights over the weekend. His organization was at a critical juncture. A few large projects worth several crores were in the pipeline. One of them was from a multinational company and faultless delivery of the project would launch them into the international scenario. It would provide them an exposure to foreign markets and get them to rub shoulders with the larger firms in the industry. Another large client he had been pursuing for the past 2 years had recently expressed an interest to go ahead with a project. If things worked out with Monalisa, he could pick up and start onboarding the clients. If it didn't and Monalisa quit, he would have to rework the pipeline and forgo most of these opportunities. That would set them back for another six to twelve months with a direct hit to the organization's top line. She was a valuable resource and he felt that understanding the situation could help him get to a solution. He wanted Monalisa to continue as part of the company.

Ayan was thirty minutes early to office, using the time to pace himself, collect his thoughts and focus on the negotiation coming up. He had spent a greater part of the weekend voiding his mind about what had happened, his assumptions about Monalisa's situation and possible outcomes from today's discussion.

Ayan had always lent himself to learning easily. He instinctively knew that despite the initial setback he wanted to turnaround the situation. He was ready to learn ways to resolve the matter, but for that he would have to probe deeper into Monalisa's mind. But, is that possible? When someone is crossed with you, how do you get into her mind? When someone does not want to negotiate, how can you get her to reveal her principal concerns and objections?

Getting to core concerns of the counterpart requires active listening. Understanding what is driving the negotiations and why the counterpart is pursuing with her actions or demands is critical before you can place your view or asks on the table. And in turn, active listening requires building a rapport with the counterpart, so that she feels safe and connected to you. Building a rapport is especially required for long term working relationships where both parties often come to the table and work side by side to deliver results. Any sentiments involved, especially the negative ones, like anger, hate, desperation, hurt, fear or horror, could hinder progress. If all parties believe that they will interact over the foreseeable future, it is imperative to adjust the negotiation style to forge a better bond. This is markedly different from one-time negotiation where both parties try to split the pie in their favor as much as possible. Relationships develop based on trust. For businesses, trust could translate into lesser expenses of money or time spent in perpetually monitoring the counterpart.

The feelings of trust and connection that emanates from the

negotiator stem from two basic tenets: voice tone and body language.

USE TONE TO CALM YOUR COUNTERPART

Your voice could set the tone for the discussion. Studies have shown that having a soothing deep voice is the most beneficial when navigating a negotiation. Think of the voice taking you through a guided mediation. A soothing deep voice conveys that you are in control but you mean no harm. It comes across as someone who is understanding and would appreciate the counterpart's point of view. It is all about what feeling you want to give off. The more you keep your voice composed, the more you diffuse strong sentiments in your counterpart. This is somewhat difficult to do in a tense situation and requires a lot of practice. Our natural urge is to scream back at the counterpart – a fight or flight reaction. Controlling the intense desire to give the counterpart a piece of our mind can and will lead to better solutions.

We once had an angry customer, Suraj Pramanick, demanding an immediate resolution. Our business was experimenting on launching a parallel wing which offered design services for customers. For any new business or project, the first few deliveries always have hiccups. The start is never smooth. Being one of our early customers, his delivery got delayed as we had underestimated the production time. He was livid that we could not deliver the project on schedule. We could see his face red with anger.

Suraj started blasting us, "Why do you take up projects when you cannot deliver?"

We were expecting this burst of anger and had prepared for this. With a sincere deep voice, I said, "We are so sorry that we have not been able to meet your expectations," starting with a confession, "We are completely responsible for the issue."

Suraj continued: "There is no point in saying sorry after you have missed the deadline. I have to answer to my stakeholders."

"We are sorry that this happened to the project. We are fully responsible for the issue," I repeated for emphasis deepening my voice even further. More than words, our brains are tuned to pick up feelings and intentions. Our brains make an intuitive assessment of the other person based on how it *feels* about the situation. A composed sincere voice conveys that you mean what you are saying. Suppose you are speaking over the phone to someone. Do you pick up how the other person feels? In most cases, yes you do. It's attributable to the tone of their voice, their pauses, and the vibes that you get over the call. You can often pick up that a person is smiling just by listening even if you aren't able to see the person on the other side.

Suraj: "I have to answer my stakeholders. What should I do now?" He let out a sigh. His anger had toned down to a great extent.

"We understand your situation. If you can give us a few more days, we will deliver the project." Next time you come across an angry counterpart, void your mind and apologize in a sincere composed voice. It may take multiple tries to get the voice right, but once you hit the right spot, you will see the counterpart release steam and give in.

What prevents us from effectively moderating our voice is the fear of rejection. Our minds are processing the responses that it can say to counter for the accusations. But more often than not, an angry counterpart just wants to be heard first. Once he has been calmed and brought to a more stable state, the deal or proceedings could be hammered out in a better way.

BODY LANGUAGE

Body language goes hand-in-hand with tone of voice. Commanding body language is indispensable in negotiations and mastering it requires a lot of practice. Here are some of the critical ones which can give you visible results in a negotiation:

1. The head nod: The simple act of nodding your head even in cases of disagreement helps communicate to your counterpart that you are listening. Maintain eye contact all through. It is a trick seasoned politicians and public figures use to portray an open attitude, defuse tension and builds association, even during touchy conversations.//
2. Your hands can betray: The part of your body that betrays the most nervousness is a shaky hand. During negotiation if you want to come across as confident and in control, then use your hands to project confidence and poise. Achieve this by keeping your arms in front of you and placing the fingertips of both hands together, spread them and then arch the palms to look like a church steeple.
3. Plant your Feet: Keeping your feet planted on the ground helps you control shaking of your legs, and in general helps hold an upright pose. If your feet are visible and you are directly in front of the counterpart, then your feet should be pointing towards your counterpart. Feet pointing to other directions signal your intent to move away from the conversation.
4. Smile and charm: Disarm your counterpart with a smile. Diffuse the tension with a smile. Especially if you are negotiating for a long term relationship, a smile signifies approachability.
5. Keep an open posture: Avoid folder arms. Lean forward to show interest in the counterpart's point of view. People want to feel heard. People want to feel that the deal is about them or includes them.
6. Show your patience: Treat negotiations as if you are explaining how a smartphone works to your grandmother. How much ever your patience is tested, maintain the composure. Keep smiling

and be with the counterpart through the deal. Especially if your counterpart has come with a lot of accusations.

1. Commit yourself to your counterpart: Don't shuffle through your notes, mobile or speak to fellow team members when your counterpart is speaking. Be all ears.

MIRRORING

Monalisa came into the office about 9:45 AM. She sat down at her desk, opened her laptop and started working. The tension was visible and the other team members had sensed it. Groups were forming around the office coffee machine trying to figure out what was happening. One thing about a botched negotiation is that more than the actual harm, it destroys the dynamics of the relationship and thus threatens to overturn any good that has been done so far. It had to be treated judiciously. Some of the team members would have, by now, started discussing about future prospects if Monalisa quit. We had to stem such discussions immediately.

Ayan called Monalisa into the cabin. She stepped in, looked at Ayan and then at me.

"It is okay. You know Mr. Datta, right? He is there to help us." Ayan said in a soothing composed voice, signaling that there was nothing to worry about.

She sat down.

Ayan continued, "I am sorry that we had a flare last day. It seems that I had retorted strongly. If you can help me understand the situation, we may be able to work out a solution."

"I feel that a solution is not possible," Monalisa said.

"A solution isn't possible?" Ayan mirrored.

"Things have gone too far out of hand. Things are not as it used to be," Monalisa leaned in and elaborated.

"It seems that you are worried that things are not the same anymore." Ayan paused.

"Yes, things are not as they used to be. There seems to be no hierarchy to the organization here. Juniors are not respecting their seniors and few old-timers are fueling this upheaval."

"Fueling the upheaval?" Ayan mirrored and leaned towards Monalisa.

Monalisa continued, revealing that team dynamics had changed over the course of the past few months. Something that Ayan had missed out entirely in his single-minded pursuit of focusing on business development. She led us into team politics that had been playing out for long to try and coup the team for personal benefits. It was getting instigated by two grieved old-timers.

Every information that Monalisa gave, Ayan continued to mirror her to find out more about the situation. Each mirror led Monalisa to reveal more information.

So, what exactly is mirroring? Mirroring is a rapport-building technique to show that you are in sync with their counterpart. It uses both verbal and non-verbal gestures to match someone's behavior. It is a persuasion technique to subtly communicate to the other person that you are listening to them and you are "like them." Mirroring happens automatically between people who know each other well. Friends, colleagues or partners tend to mirror each other not only in voice, style, tempo, body language but also in dressing sense, choice of movies and selection of food. It is meant to show that "I am like you" when it happens consciously.

Mirroring was accidentally discovered by a team of researchers in Italy led by Giacomo Rizzolatti, a neuroscientist at the University of Parma. The researchers were doing some experiments on monkeys. These experiments required monkeys to sit in a specially designed laboratory chair, get their head and other body parts wired up and be connected to a

Active Listening

monitor. This monitor was configured to beep whenever some part of the monkey's brain would fire up during the process. Just before beginning of one such round of experiment, a monkey was waiting in the chair with all the wiring setup and the researcher yet to begin. During this wait, one of the researchers walked in and casually grabbed her food from the table and the monitor beeped. Even though the monkey's hand hadn't moved, its brain had reciprocated the researcher's hand, as if it had grabbed the food even without actually doing so. Even more surprisingly, it was the same region of the brain that would also lit up when the monkey itself grabbed the food. Series of experiments later, it was established that the monkey's brain contained special cells known as "mirror neurons", which fired whenever it saw or heard an action.

It turns out that mirror neurons in humans are smarter, flexible and more highly evolved than the monkeys. Human beings are social creatures and survival depends on understanding the actions, intentions, and nuances of others. These neurons allow us to comprehend the minds of others not through reasoning but through simulation – through feeling and not through thinking.

Simulated mirroring in negotiation can be used to echo our natural tendencies to mirror. Research has shown that mirroring, when done right, could lead to successful outcomes.

Mirroring body language is mimicking the gestures of the counterpart like chin rubbing, leaning on one side of the chair, sitting upright, crossing legs or playing with the hair. Body language mirroring needs to be subtle with no sudden jerks or transitions. For example, if your counterpart sitting upright shifts his stance to lean on one arm of the chair and you make a sudden move to mirror it, it will look contrived. But if you ease it out, as if you are adjusting yourself in the chair and then mirror, it will look more natural. Ensure there is a gap of a few seconds before you start the mirroring process. Remember, if done forcefully or it doesn't look natural, your counterpart will sense it and this technique will backfire.

If a boss wants to create a rapport with a nervous employee, he can mirror his employee's posture. If an employee needs to get a favor from her boss, she can use the mirroring technique to replicate his body language to show that she is in sync with him. However, a word of caution when mirroring body language of people up the chain. Don't mirror body language which inherently shows superiority, like locking your fingers and placing them at the back of your head; or leaning back in the chair with legs crossed.

VERBAL MIRRORING

Verbal mirroring can be used for both face to face or telephonic negotiations. The concept of verbal mirroring is ludicrously simple.

Repeat back the last (or the most crucial) three or four words with a question mark. For example, Ayan said "A solution isn't possible?" and "fueling the upheaval?" When delivered in a composed inquisitive tone, it feels like you are asking for more clarity and not questioning the counterpart. You just have to deliver in a sincere tone. In a natural setting, this format is meant to seek more clarification from the counterpart regarding what was just said. What a verbal mirroring does is trigger the counterpart to explain and provide more information on what she had just said. This would unearth potentially more critical and deeper concerns or provide decisive data that you, as a negotiator, can employ in framing your demands.

I had known for a long time that mirroring works in general to build rapport with people, but never felt that it could form a part of my negotiation arsenal to unearth more information. One day, I was waiting in the lobby to meet a new client and I overheard two office employees discussing a deal they were navigating with a client.

"Hey, I got late for lunch today. Was on call with a client for the

Active Listening

Express Project."

"Express Project?"

"Yeah, the one where we have to develop a management software. It's has a large number of input sources and I can't get the client to give me a proper structure to start the project. Not sure how we can deliver the project on time."

"It seems that the client is really tough to work with."

"Yeah! Clients do not understand that unless we have clarity on the entire data flow, we cannot have a succinct software. I had told them to give the details two weeks back, but they haven't delivered yet."

"They haven't delivered yet?"

"No, I have lost two weeks with no progress on the project. This will put our team in a needlessly compelling situation when the delivery dates come due. I have to tell my boss that we need more time."

"More time?"

"Yes, I think we need to extend the project another 4 weeks or so. I will be going to meet him today evening."

Look at the flow. It is natural. It is about understanding the other person. It is becoming all ears about what the other person has to say. It is about their feelings. Parroting the words as spoken assures the listener that they have been heard. It encourages the counterpart to reflect, go deeper inside their own minds and find out why they said what they said.

And in parallel, notice one crucial point. We came to know about what problems this employee was facing with the client. But did you get to know anything about the other person? No, right? That's the beauty of using the right mirrors. You can get all the information you want without sharing much about your position - which is crucial in a negotiation. You want to know as much as possible about your counterpart but revealing as little as possible about yourself.

GETTING YOUR AUDIENCE TO FEEL ENGAGED

If you are a coach or trainer, you can use the mirroring technique to get your audience to feel connected and understood. At the beginning of the session, ask them what they expect from the session. Then use mirrors to repeat back what they just said. The audience or participants will provide more insights into their asks and in turn reveal their actual wants. This can continue as long as you want or till you feel that you have got to the core.

7-38-55 RULE

To get Monalisa to open up, Ayan's spoken words had to be in sync with his tone of voice and body language. His way of leaning forward and speaking in a soothing composed voice provided the nurturing atmosphere and psychological security for her to open up. The relative significance of spoken words, tone of voice and body language is captured in the 7-38-55 rule.

7-38-55 rule states that 7% of the meaning in a communication is through the words spoken, 38% through tone of voice and 55% through body language. What this means is that the content or words spoken will contribute only 7% of the meaning and it will be interpreted only in the context of tone of voice and body language which contributes a massive 93% of the meaning (38% + 55% = 93%). For example, the question "What do you mean?" means differently depending on the way it was spoken and body language used. A very aggressive loud accusatory tone with fists thumping on the table portrays anger and frustration. Whereas, the same words spoken in a soft inquisitive tone with an easy-going body language portrays an eagerness to learn more about the topic.

In negotiations, whether it is you who is speaking or interpreting your counterpart who is speaking, 93% of the perception will emanate from tone and body language. Non-verbal signals and body movements convey or reveal much more in any negotiation than actual words that

Active Listening

are spoken.

If at any point during the negotiation, you are only listening to the words without looking for clues in the non-verbal channel, you are at a high risk of misinterpreting what your counterpart is meaning. Find below four strategic rules to apply in a negotiation context:

1. Their body language signals how much they are in harmony with you: If the counterpart's body language is not in sync with what you are saying and indicates that they might be losing you, slow down whatever you are saying and take few steps back. Rephrase whatever you have just conveyed and clarify their queries before moving on. Conversely if their body language signals that they do not believe you are listening to them, then they may not proceed to reveal much information. Use a comforting tone of voice and an immersive body language to get your counterpart to trust you.

2. Seek inconsistencies between their non-verbal cues and spoken words: When your counterpart is speaking, find out if their non-verbal cues match the words they are saying. If someone is saying "I am interested in..." while at the same time their body language signals withdrawal from the discussion, it is an indication that something is amiss and needs to be investigated. Similarly, if you are not keeping eye-contact, your counterpart will read it as insecurity no matter what you say.

3. Use tonality to suit the negotiation: Your tone signals how your counterpart will receive the words. If your counterpart is aggressive and you are using an aggressive tone to prove your point, it will result in unnecessary conflicts. Depending on the impression that you want to give to your counterparts, change your throw of voice. This is specifically true when you are asking questions - you would want to sound sincerely concerned rather than make it look like an interrogation. Use the composed tone

of voice to sound respectful and genuine.

4. Present coherent non-verbal signals: Your counterpart will be responding more to the body language and tone of your voice rather than the words spoken. Depending on what you want to convey, portray the correct signals or alter your demeanor based on the signals what you receive from the counterpart. Even if the nature of your arguments does not change, a change in non-verbal signals will do the work.

As you will discover, this book places a lot of stress in the way words are spoken in tandem with the actual content. If a stressful negotiation comes your way, a comforting tone of voice and an accommodating body language will calm down the counterpart and reveal what they really want.

FLIPPING

Ayan had been going well with Monalisa. He was driving to the root cause of the problem, but more importantly he was hearing out Monalisa. We could see her softening bit by bit; her body language had moved from tensed to eased to relaxed. Her jaw muscles had relaxed, shoulders softened, her furrowed eyebrow eased. She felt heard. She felt important. But of all, she felt that she was still respected in the organization. That she was valued by Ayan.

The rest of the office was getting jumpy. It was about 11 AM now. They needed to know. We wanted to know. We needed to get to a conclusion quickly. But one thing about negotiations is that the moment you feel pressured to conclude it with a deadline, you have lost. If as a negotiator you feel trapped in a timeframe, it would be time to shift the frame or diffuse the deadline.

Ayan looked at Monalisa asked if she would like some water. He got up and went to the pantry. It allowed her to take a break. The cloud

Active Listening

in her mind had started to dissipate. She was thinking more clearly. She was exercising judgement. She was open to finding a solution. There is a saying that never make a decision when you're angry. Calming her helped the cause.

"Here you go," Ayan handed over the glass of water to her.

She raised the glass to her lips, stopped midway and asked, "What do you think I should do?"

Ayan was caught off-guard. He hadn't expected Monalisa would ask for his opinion. At the least so soon. That is the beauty of active listening. You will keep getting surprised at what you can unearth.

Ayan centered himself. We had discussed this over the weekend. He knew what to say. "That is something I am also trying to find an answer to. What do you think you should do?"

Monalisa: "I am not sure. After so many years in the company, it is difficult for me to stand such transgressions. I don't know what path to take from here."

Ayan mirrored, "Path from here?"

Monalisa: "I have broached the idea of quitting the job after a lot of thought. Do you feel that I should continue here?"

Ayan: "I wanted to get your views on that. If we work out something internally, do you feel that you can continue?"

Monalisa: "I guess I can."

Ayan smiled after a long time.

Two weeks later and after a detailed internal investigation, Ayan terminated two of his employees found guilty of misconduct. Two more were given a warning.

Flipping is like the Judo in communication. Judo (Japanese for "the gentle way") is a modern martial art which emphasis winning by using the counterpart's energy to work on your behalf while preserving your own mental and physical energy. It embodies that good techniques can win over sheer strength. There are no kicks or punches. Like Judo, flipping gets you to direct the counterpart's energy and gets them to work for you.

The basic premise of flipping is to answer a question with a question. It is that simple. In doing so, you stay at the periphery, you get more information and start to approach the underlying motivation behind the counterpart's questions. When you flip, you build rapport by helping the counterpart focus on the thing dearest to her – herself. You are channeling her thoughts in the flip direction.

Three things to keep in mind while flipping:

One, only flip at appropriate times. Don't use this as an elixir for all questions asked by your counterpart. Some questions do not lend themselves to flipping, like "What time is it?" or "How do I get to the station?". Use it specifically to get more information about their underlying assumptions.

Two, have a goal in mind. What is that you are trying to reach? What hypothesis are you trying to validate? What information are you looking to collect? For example, in a sales call, if the client asks "How big is your company?", you can flip it with "That is an important question. When you say big, are you referring to revenues, employees, clientele or impact on the industry?"

Three, use a softening pre-phrase with the flip. Prefix with a statement that places the flip in a humble sincere tone. The softening statement cushions the impact of the flip and makes it sound less harsh. See for yourself how stark it sounds in the above example if we did not use a softening statement. "That is an important question. When you say big, are you referring to revenues, employees, clientele or impact on the industry?" versus "What do you want to know about the company?"

Active Listening

Look at how Ayan flipped Monalisa's questions "What do you think I should do?" using "What do you think you should do?" He then proceeds to use a mirror to get her to open up more. Then he again flips with "Do you feel that you can continue?" At each step, she gives away what she really wants to do. It may be the case that even your counterpart is not aware of her innate wants. Mirroring and flipping also helps to clarify herself to herself.

Here are some more examples of flipping:

"Thanks for the presentation. What is the cost of this service?" --- "Thank you for listening to our presentation. We can help you if you can guide us what is the number of employees for whom you would deploy the solution."

"When can you deliver the products?" --- "Yes, that is what we were coming to. Do you have an internal deadline for this?"

"How will this help me?" --- "That is a good question. Before we get into that, can you help us understand your biggest challenges?"

"Your price is too high. Can you bring down the price?" --- "We will come to that in a bit. What is the price range you are looking for?"

BLOCKING

Sometimes you wouldn't want to give away more information to the client. You would simply want to dig more, not the other way around. However, there may be some questions that you cannot avoid answering. You can try and block those.

Blocking is to answer your counterpart without actually answering the question. It is a pseudo answer. It is a no-stakes answer.

Remember the lead from an earlier chapter who was posh and had asked "How much will this cost me to take up?". Our reply was "this one is expensive."

That is a block. The lead felt he got an answer to his question, but 'expensive' is not something concrete. The information that you have shared is not worth much. Your counterpart will not notice this subtlety and interpret your answer in their way.

Here are some examples of blocking:

"At what frequency do you update your software with patches." --- "We update it regularly."

"How quickly can you ramp up the production?" --- "We are working on it. You will see the results shortly."

"We have a new product. Can I visit your office to give a demo?" --- "Give us some days."

"What is the cost of this product?" --- "A lot"

Blocking satisfies the necessity of an answer without revealing much information or the information that you are giving is not much worth. Most of the time the counterpart will not notice it but will satisfy their quest. Or, assume what they want to believe, true or otherwise, and carry on with the negotiation.

SPOTTING LIARS

In negotiations, it may be necessary to spot liars. Lying in a negotiation can be an outright lie or deliberate omission of facts. Outright lies or lies by commission are those where the counterpart blatantly tells a lie on the face. Lies by omission are those where the counterpart evades the question or suppresses facts deliberately. Most people admit to having lied in negotiations to get what they wanted. And almost everyone believes that they have been told lies during negotiations.

The process of negotiation by itself is dynamic and uneven and navigating the terrain itself is difficult. And to that, if we add liars, then it becomes all the more complex and exhausting. Often, in a negotiation we cannot ask the counterpart to repeat everything they just said and

Active Listening

look them in the eye to detect pupil dilation or other tell-tale signs of a lie. Visual cues can be used to detect a lie but many times registering a visual cue at a fraction of a second may not always be possible. An easier and effective technique may be in the words spoken by the counterpart.

An experiment conducted by researchers have found clues to detect signs of lying, which then can be used to further investigate the counterpart. This experiment was called the ultimatum game, in which participants were divided into pairs. One of them was the allocator and the other person was the receiver. The allocator was given a sum of money and was told to share a portion of the money to the receiver. If the receiver agreed to the split, then both of them would keep the money as per the split. If the receiver rejected the split, then the entire amount would be withdrawn by the researcher and neither the allocator nor the receiver will get any amount.

Suppose for example, the total amount given to the allocator was INR 10 and the allocator gave INR 7 to the receiver. If the receiver agreed to the split, the allocator will keep INR 3 and the receiver will get INR 7. But if the receiver disagreed, the entire INR 10 would be given back to the researcher.

There was a small twist here. The amount initially handed over by the experimenter to the allocator was not disclosed to the receiver. The allocator could receive a large amount, say INR 100 or a small amount INR 20. And the receiver had no direct way of finding out how much the allocator had got. The receiver had to make a decision based on listening to answers and clarifications that the allocator gave to the receiver.

After the series of experiments were over, the researchers found that seventy percent of the allocators were honest and told the receivers the total amount they initially got. Remaining thirty percent lied by omission or by commission. They also found the following:

1. Liars used more words: Blatant liars or those who lied by

commission used many more words than truth-tellers. They felt that they needed to justify their stance more to make up for the lie. The number of words grew with the lie.

2. Liars used more swear words than truth-tellers. This was an expressive response to the stress of lying and the liars did not have enough mental energy left to control the nature of words being spoken. This was especially true when the receiver voiced their suspicion about the actual amount initially given to the allocator by the researcher.

3. Liars used a lot more third person to distance themselves from the lie and avoid ownership of what they were saying. They used words like he, him, his, himself, she, her, hers, herself, it, its, itself, they, them, their, theirs, and themselves.

4. Liars used more complex sentences rather than simple ones, probably in an attempt to mask and complicate the truth.

The next time when in a negotiation you find any of these factors, it is a sign that the counterpart has to be probed more. These are not foolproof but can be used as a cautionary approach to get more information and listen more intently.

CHAPTER SUMMARY

Listening is a magic skill that can transform the trajectory of any negotiation. The best negotiators get their counterparts talking. They gently nudge their counterpart to reveal more. They try to unearth as much information as possible from the counterpart – information that could alter the deal-making process. Consciously or unconsciously the counterpart holds information that is valuable to you.

Listen, Listen, and then listen some more. Your goal is to be an active listener and absorb anything that comes out from your counterpart's mouth. You do not need to respond to whether they are correct or

Active Listening

otherwise. Here are the key takeaways from the chapter:

- Mirroring gets you into your counterpart's mind. It tells them that you are listening intently and empathizing with them. Use mirrors to get your counterpart to talk more, give more clarification and give you more time to think

- To use mirrors, repeat the last few words or the critical few words in the statement what the counterpart has just made. Pause after each mirror to let the counterpart process and elaborate on what they just said.

- Use a soothing and composed tone. Your mirrors should look like requests and clarifications rather than interrogation. Keep you pitch low and try for a deeper voice. Speak slowly and clearly.

- Have a positive body language in tandem with what you are talking. Use head nods and open arms to convey to your counterpart that you are listening. Have a smile always – it relaxed the counterpart and diffuses any tension in the discussions. Even over the phone, smile when speaking. The person on the other end of the line can pick up the smiling vibe.

- Body language mirroring shows you are in sync with your counterpart. It works marvelously if used subtly. Copy their body language only to the extent socially possible or only till it doesn't seem too loud.

- Remember 7-38-55 rule: Your spoken words are just 7% of the meaning, the rest 93% is dependent on your tone of voice and body language. More than the actual words being spoken, your counterpart will act on the non-verbal signals.

- Use flipping to get your counterpart to answer their own questions. If you don't have an immediate answer or you want to keep them speaking, flip the question and learn about what they feel should be answer to the question they asked.

- Blocking is satisfying the need for an answer without giving out much information. Sometimes, you would be required to answer, but it may be too early to share anything specific to the counterpart. Use vague answers like "costly", "more time", "soon", "from someone." Your attempt to skirt the question by using blocking will not even be noticed by the counterpart.

- Listening intently can help you become more cautious about potential liars. Liars in general use more words and complex sentences or using third-person pronouns like he, him, himself, they them, their and so on. This can be used as a signal to probe further and listen more intently.

DYNAMIC SILENCE

Avijit's mind was racing. The meeting was scheduled at 3 PM. It was 2nd June 2014. A typical hot summer afternoon in India. He checked the documents, picked up his diary, tucked his pen in the shirt pocket and walked down the office steps towards the car.

Avijit Mukherjee was the human resource head for Shreyian Packaging. It was a mid-sized company with about 150 workers. It manufactured packing materials including but not limited to boxes, printed films and laminated pouches distributed across India from their manufacturing-cum-warehousing unit in Dhulagarh. The company had grown from a 6-member team about 10 years back to 150-member team with a sales presence in 17 states across India. It had withstood the economic downturn of 2009-10 and emerged as a leader in the packaging industry from Eastern India. Senior management had just allocated a budget for setting up another manufacturing unit to keep up with the intensifying demand.

Avijit was on his way to meet Surya, the elected representative of the workers' union. They had been working together for the past five years ensuring that both the company goals and employee demands were met. They shared more than a strong working relationship. They respected each other's stand and hammered out issues in a mutually acceptable way.

Surya had been with the company for 8 years. He had joined when the company was shifting its base from Howrah to Dhulagarh. He had been instrumental in helping the company set up this manufacturing unit following the latest standards. He had been promoting employee welfare and ensuring that issues like employee safety, allowances, cultural programs and medical facilities were raised to the management team from time to time.

But over the last three months, the equation had degenerated. It was the result of a miscommunication between management and union over the sacking of 3 workers on productivity grounds. That was a sensitive issue where the management had to take a hard call. Something that had not gone down well with the workers.

About a month earlier, the company had asked to increase the worker duty hours by 2 hours to cope up with the demand. It was proposed as a temporary measure till the time the new manufacturing unit came up. Avijit and Surya had been under tremendous pressure from their sides to work out a solution. Every passing day the company was losing out on fulfilling new demands. The production could not keep up with sales. The management had been pushing Avjiit to make this effective as quickly as possible. This would also require changes in work schedule, production flow and employee productivity.

Avijit reached out to Surya about few days back asking for a meet in a neutral place. There would be one more representative from each side. Priya accompanied Avijit, while Bhavesh accompanies Surya.

Surya and Bhavesh had just reached. After exchanging pleasantries, Surya said, "Let us get down to the issue."

"I am sorry I have been pushing you hard for this change. The company wants to implement the new work schedule as quickly as possible. There are lot of market factors in play here. The competition has already started eating into our orders because we have not been able to fulfill them. Plus, our channel partners may start losing faith in our manufacturing capabilities if we cannot replenish their stocks urgently. There is also the peak season coming up and we would not want to lose out on peak demand. Have you been able to discuss this with the workers?" Avijit asked.

"No, a majority is against the move."

"Against the move?" Avijit mirrored.

"Yes, against the move. A majority does not want to go ahead. They are having reservations with the new extended work hours. It is difficult for me to push the case in such a scenario."

Surya was divided in thought. While a part of the workforce was understanding of the situation, but the majority was against the move. He had been discussing with them but could not agree to a solution internally. Surya could not lose the backing of the majority. When they had stayed with him in every way, he also had to support them whenever required. A forced change could mean losing out on the workers' confidence.

Avijit also wanted Surya to continue as the elected representative. Surya was sympathetic towards the management's goals and wanted that truce always prevailed. He was also a work-first leader with a strong work ethic and wanted that an equilibrium is maintained at all times to ensure productivity. But off late, there was an opposing faction building up amongst the workers trying to topple Surya. That would be a massacre for the company as their views were highly contrarian and destructive to the company's objective.

"Help me understand why this is so," asked Avijit

"They are reserved against the idea of extending the work hours."

"This is a temporary arrangement till the other manufacturing unit goes live," Avijit offered clarification.

"See, the new unit has been just commissioned! Even the basic foundation has not started. I was there when the existing operational unit was being built. I know that there will be challenges along the way. It is not easy to stick to deadlines in this market conditions. There will be delays and the new setup may not even start within the next 12 months. And even if it starts, ramping up the production will take time. A lot of time. Workers feel that it will take at least 18 months. How long do you think it will take to start production?" asked Surya.

"That is a good question. We are in discussion with the contractor to get it ready as soon as possible. But for exact deadlines, I have to check that with management. For how long do you think the workers can work on this extended schedule?" said Avijit flipping the question.

"The workers are concerned that this arrangement may become the norm going forward. Plus, with the festive season some months away, some of them would be going back to their home towns."

"And…" chimed in Avijit and paused.

Surya blinked. "And they are concerned that they will not be able to work overtime for a continuous period of 18 months. That this will impact their health and wellbeing. It is a strenuous job working. Workers sweat it out every day in the sweltering heat," he responded.

"We really appreciate you letting us know how the workmen feel. They are part of the big family and we wouldn't take any step if it causes them harm. How can we can work things out here?" Avijit leaned forward silently to listen. Surya looked sideways towards Bhavesh as if seeking consent to continue.

"Avijit, I can convince the workers for a rotational overtime shift if you can work out an improved medical policy and a higher overtime pay for this arrangement."

"Higher overtime pay?" Avijit mirrored.

"Yes, given the current scenario, the workers would need an increase of at least 15% over the standard overtime rate."

Avijit stared into Surya with a blank look on his face. There was a long silence.

Surya continued, "I know what I am asking is high. But given the circumstances we cannot do anything." He then paused as if what he just said didn't make sense. Avijit let the pause linger. It was an uneasy vacuum.

Surya shifted in his seat as if negotiating with himself. He broke the quietness. "Nothing less than an 8% increment and overtime on a rotational basis. I won't commit anything now, but I will speak to the workers for consideration. I need their buy-in."

Anything that isn't an upfront reject is one further step in the negotiation. And, without saying a word or giving a counteroffer, Avijit had halved the incremental overtime payout.

A very aggressive tool in a negotiator's arsenal is the dynamic silence. It is a powerful tool which when used correctly can topple negotiations in our favor. Silence is giving a strategic pause, causing a void in the communication. We tend to think of silences as negative. Human beings tend to see silences as a failure to move the negotiation ahead and rush to fill them quickly. It forces your counterpart to jump in and say something. Silence is uncomfortable and awkward. However, when used properly and strategically, silence turns into dynamic silence and can work charmingly for a negotiator.

THE RIGHT WAY TO USE SILENCE

Dynamic silence is brilliant. When used in a negotiation, the counterpart gets nervous and proceeds to dig a hole for themselves.

The first way to use silence is to use it as a prod. While this version of the technique is less effective than what its practitioners would like to believe, it is still a decent way to start with inexperienced counterparts. Most people, although not everyone, feel uncomfortable with silence in conversation. They speak into the silence, to fill it and will do so without much cajoling. So, some passive-aggressive negotiators use this technique to exploit our inherent nature by opening up long, uneasy silences. By being silent and without engaging, they can apply indirect pressure that would be harder to generate using words. With this raw technique, untrained negotiators are manipulated into speaking without thinking, spilling more information than they should or even negotiating against themselves. This works but often leads to unproductive negotiations. Long bouts of silence can make the counterpart defensive and spoil the relation.

The second way is to be subtle in its use. It is much more effective and cuts through to the core. Use silence as a way to coax the counterpart into saying more than they planned to, rather than prodding them. Instead of a long awkward silence, a trained negotiator waits for the right time to be silent. Often he does so just after a mirror, a flip or a connector. Something which forces the audience to open up more and clarify. The tone has to be a conversational one. There are four steps if you want to milk more information from your counterpart:

1. Start with a sincere composed tone
2. Use a mirror, flip or a connector
3. Pause, for at least 3 to 4 seconds
4. Repeat as often as required.

To be effective and not burn bridges, silence has to be short. Ideally the counterpart shouldn't know that the negotiator is using it. This makes it a helpful tactic for low-pressure negotiations, intended to get more information efficiently than asking direct questions. Use this with a mirror, flip or a connector; just when the counterpart is finishing a statement to subtly signal them to continue. If you want to get your counterpart to negotiate against themselves, use the silence with a softening phrase.

THE STARING CONTENT

I discovered the importance of silence early in my career. My boss used to schedule random meetings on afternoons. He would call me in his office, ask me to sit down and stare at me.

Silence. Stare. More silence.

Being a newbie in the company, I used to get jittery and start blabbering on topics which I felt maybe the cause of getting called into the cabin. This used to happen often. After several such occurrences, I confided with a senior on this. He revealed that I wasn't the only one on whom the silence treatment was getting dealt. Many before me had gone through the process.

Let me tell you, it's not easy at all to shield against this trick. Human beings by nature want to connect to others. We are social beings. We just can't resist the urge to communicate. It took me a couple of months to master the trick. After that, instead of starting to blabber even before I hit the chair, I just sat down and stared back at my boss. After all, it wasn't me who called the meeting.

It was comical to see my boss's face. He never tried this trick again on me.

HOW CLOSE.IO SAVED MONEY

Steli Efti is the CEO of Saas sales software Close.io. In the initial years, the founding team of the company were doing something completely different. They started with a service that allowed customers to sign up with their banking cards to have Close.io round up all their transactions and donate the change to charity. For this to happen, the team had bought a technology license from a third party under a three-year contract.

With little foresight about the future direction of the company, the Close.io team had negotiated a special agreement with the technology company. In the first year, they would pay nothing. In the second year, they would have a bit more. The third year would be when they would make the bulk of the payment – close to 90% of the deal value.

The founding team had assumed that in three years they would either be crazy-successful or out of business, so either way it did not matter. If they were successful, paying the bulk contract value in the third year would be a breeze. If they were out of business, it didn't matter that the contract was live.

About one year in, the team pivoted to a new business model. They now did not require the licensed technology and were not willing to fund the contract anymore.

It was a grave situation – the team wanted to direct the money to critical requirements of the new business model and not spend on a dead contract. After some cajoling and speaking to a board member of the technology company, they got an account representative to listen to their issue.

The account representative called saying that they had discussed this internally and since Close.io was a startup; instead of the actual payment of $250000, they could reduce the payment to $100000 and absolve them from the contract.

That was a huge burden off the startup's shoulder. Steli had reduced liability worth $125000 over the call. But she wanted to press more. Instead of negotiating with a number, she kept quiet.

The account representative could not take the silence. After a few awkward seconds, he filled in the silence. He said that if they waited for a couple of more months, he could reduce the payment to $25000-$50000 range.

Steli agreed. In just a few minutes' call, her obligation reduced from $250000 to $25000 – a reduction of $225000. That is a sizable sum of money. That would probably not have been possible if Steli had countered with a number.

This is what Steli had to say about the deal: "Nine out of ten times, keeping your mouth shut at the right moment will work better than anything 'clever' you could ever say."

THE INADVERTENT SILENT TREATMENT

A friend of mine wanted to purchase a second-hand cabinet. After going through a popular online marketplace for pre-owned furniture, he finalized on a cabinet which was the right size for this room. It was a dark brown laminated TV cum bookshelf styled cabinet with exquisite designs on the front panel. It matched the room interiors and added an artistic feel to it. She called up the seller asking for the price.

The seller said he couldn't go less than INR 30000 for it. Being beyond budget, my friend panicked and put down the phone abruptly. The seller called back a couple of days later with an offer price of INR 19000, which my friend agreed. Was she savvy? Gosh, no! Far from that, she panicked because she hadn't estimated it to cost that much. To this day, whenever I visit her house, the cabinet reminds me of the importance of silence in life and negotiations.

Silence goes hand-in-hand with the chapter on need versus want. To be silent is to say that you do not need this deal. To be silent is to affirm that you are in charge.

HOW TO RAISE A RAISE?

We couldn't have been more proud than how Subham, a participant from one of our coaching sessions, used silence to raise a raise he had already got.

Subham had been with the company for 3 years looking after Eastern Region Operations. He had been expecting a promotion now. He had joined the company as Assistant Manager and it was time for the year-end review. As per the company process, before discussion with his manager, Subham had filled up an online feedback questionnaire. This year had been especially good for him. He had helped his company save on costs of up to INR 20 Lakhs through digitization. He had spearheaded the campaign and coordinated across departments to make this possible. With less physical documentation, the company not only saved direct costs, but also increased productivity and employee morale.

Subham got called into his manager's cabin.

"Hello Subham, sit down," his manager smiled and pointed to a chair.

"Thank you Sir," Subham replied.

"So, you have done wonderfully this year. You have saved on some company cost. That is commendable. Nice work."

"Thank you Sir. It would not have been possible without your encouragement. You have helped in moving past obstacles and guiding me all through." These words never fail to work. You can't get this wrong if the delivery is genuine.

"To reward your commitment to the company, we are offering you a promotion to the post of Deputy Manager." His boss extended his hands. Subham took them and shook hard. He had been expecting this for some time now.

"Thank you once again for considering me for promotion," Subham replied.

"There is another good news for you. You have got an increment of

14% this year," smiled his boss.

Subham had participated in our coaching sessions a couple of months back. He found this opportunity to be just right to practice the silence tactic. Negotiating verbally may lead to counteroffers. So he let his boss play out the negotiation in his head.

Subham genuinely smiled and kept silent. It was as if he expected his boss to say something more. His boss shifted in his seat. His boss was negotiating with himself. Was the number he gave too low? Was Subham expecting more? Can he put together a bit more given Subham's contribution to the company? Finally, after a few seconds, he said, "I can go up to 19% increment for you."

And to save face, his boss added, "and this is just because you have been valuable to the company."

"Thank you Sir. The project would not have been complete without your support," Subham softened the effects of the awkward silence. As he got up to leave, his boss said, "Don't mention the increment number to anyone."

Not bad a return on investment for Subham on a negotiation coaching he attended two months back.

HOW TO DEFLECT IF SILENCE IS USED ON YOU?

What if someone used this tactic on you? Either because he is a trained negotiator or because the skills come effortlessly to him. You have been drawn into a spontaneous conversation through active listening and silence. How do you deflect? Even if you are trained, this technique falls below our cognitive threshold and hence you will not always be able to detect its use. Very few will be able to reliably recognize this tactic and say nothing. It is helpful to have more active strategies to resist the dynamic silence.

Take a notebook and pen with you to every negotiation meeting.

When done with your end of the response, cultivate a habit of taking notes. Write down the discussion or other details giving you some time to think. Or, pick up the glass of water and start taking small sips.

Alternatively, you can ask a question to your counterpart related to what you just said or the last thing that the other side put in the conversation. When asking questions, do not rush to reframe your question? Or worse still, answer your own question if the counterpart still remains silent. Use silence even in these small moments rather than feeling the need to talk.

Finally, Practice, practice and practice.

Silence is a tough skill to conquer. It is aggressive. It is uncompromising. Many negotiators are unwilling to even try it. Silence should not be used as a pressurizing tactic, and the counterpart should not even recognize that you're using this tool. It is most effective when it is delicate and used with softening phrases before or after the technique is deployed. It has the power to reshape negotiations and extract startling information while leaving counterparties with the impression that they are in charge of the discussion.

CHAPTER SUMMARY

A lot of negotiation advice focuses on what to say and how to say. We focus on how to begin the conversation and the best ways to communicate our words and demands from the discussion. With this mindset, we lose focus on a very powerful tool that negotiators can use during the discussion. Dynamic silence is when you strategically insert silence in the discussion to force your counterpart to fill in the void. It has to be used with other techniques given in the book.

Here are the key takeaways from this chapter:

- Use the dynamic silence to force your counterpart to speak.
- On way to use silence is to use it as a prodding device and a

Dynamic Silence

pressure tactic. Human beings are prone to talk more and express themselves. Whenever they find silence, they start speaking. And the more your counterpart speaks the more information they are divulging. When prodding, you can open up the conversation by just forcing silence in the discussion. However, this may backfire as the counterpart can see these as manipulative and devious.

- The better way to use silence is to use it with other techniques given in the book, like mirroring or flipping the question. Ask a question or mirror and give a brief pause of 3-4 seconds to let the words sink in. Let the dynamic silence flow smoothly with the conversation. Make it more natural.

- Deflect silence if it is used on you. Take a notebook and pen and after you are over with your statement start taking notes. This focuses you to do something else and yet deflects the need to fill the silence. Alternatively start taking small sips of water.

- It is a tough skill to acquire. It is not natural to remain silent for long times, especially for people who are extroverts or aggressive. They tend to see silence as permission to speak. Curb your desire and let the counterpart take the bait.

DIG DEEPER

Piyali was tensed. She had been wanting to speak to her mother on this subject for quite some time. Being the Principal Consultant at a multinational consulting firm, the nature of her job often led her to travel outside her home town for days at a stretch. Some days she would return via an evening flight and leave early morning next day. Amid all of this, she has been struggling to get her diabetic mother to exercise regularly. Her mother, like most mothers, seemed to never heed what Piyali was saying. She would either give some excuse or justify her regular household chores as an alternate to the prescribed exercises. She always missed her schedules.

As many of you may have encountered, negotiating with parents is one of the toughest; one where your self-discipline and patience are most tested. And one which is most fraught with sentiments. The doctor, apart from prescribing drugs had strictly asked Piyali's mother to continue physical activity regularly. At least two and a half hours of moderate-intensity physical activity per week. It was difficult for Piyali to continuously keep track of her mother's dietary and fitness regimen amid the taut workload. And every time she came back home after travel, she found out that her mother did not follow through on either of those regimens.

Piyali was exasperated. It was a big headache for Piyali. Every passing day for a diabetic patient is like a ticking time bomb. A sudden change in sugar levels could lead to an emergency. And with her being away from home for many days a month, this would mean disaster. Maintaining diet and regular exercise have shown to be effective and could stall the deterioration to a great extent.

One Sunday afternoon, Piyali confronted her mother. "Mother, you need to strictly follow the exercise and diet plan. You don't understand how important this is."

Her mother shooed her away, "I don't want to go through these conversations again. I am doing the best I can do. That's all. Now will you let me continue reading my book?" She picked up her book and looked away.

"See mother, studies have shown that regular physical activity improves blood glucose control and can prevent or delay type 2 diabetes. Physical activity and modest weight loss have been shown to lower type 2 diabetes risk by up to 58% in high-risk patients."

"I really don't want to discuss any further. It is stressful for me. I am not going to talk about this anymore."

"The first few weeks are most difficult for any change. But once you keep doing it for 21 days, you will get used to it. You have to understand that exercising is very important for you."

The discussion was going nowhere. Piyali was frustrated. The conversation always ended on the same predictable path. All her efforts fell on deaf ears. She felt powerless and dejected. Should she be more assertive next time? Should she engage instructors to come home regularly and get her mother to do the exercises? How will she manage her dieting regimens?

Have you ever had a similar futile discussion trying to get someone to see your side of the arguments but failed? I bet you have. You would have tried to logically prove your point, but in vain. You would have provided all necessary information which solidifies your opinions but to no avail. You would have failed to get a commitment from the counterpart.

The truth is that arguments and sound logic is only a small part in the negotiation process. Trapping the counterpart with logic will not get them to sign a deal, or buy a house, or go for exercising.

Standard economic theory assumes that human beings are skilled in making rational choices and that markets and institutions are healthily self-regulating. Those of us who went through basic economics were taught that human beings are rational beings and they are expected to behave rationally all through. Most individuals approach negotiations by separating emotions from the person. They believe that emotions do more harm than good at the negotiations table and separating them from the equation leads to a better-balanced result. We often hear things like "Keeping the emotions aside, this is …". They believe that different people have different emotions and negotiators should keep emotions away from the discussion. They believe that emotions often create fear or anger and hence they should be detached from the person.

Logic has its place in negotiation. Rigorous preparation is critical in any negotiation. The bigger and more important the transaction the more important it is to identify core issues, interest, fallback options, and gauge how the counterpart looks at the negotiation. Both parties have to pull up data and research the market before coming to the negotiation table. So is determining walkaway options in case the deal falls through.

But that is only half the story.

Think of this for a moment. Negotiation is a high-stakes game. Everyone who comes to the negotiating table is always charged up to

Dig Deeper

some extent. You cannot separate emotions from a person. The truth is that emotions matter in negotiations and dispute resolution. You need to be able to grasp and understand the emotional undercurrent in the situation and how that is getting played out throughout the negotiation. At the basic level, these may be resentments (like that of an angry customer) or anxieties (like asking your boss for a salary raise) or fear (like losing out on a deal) or excitement (like coming across a massive revenue opportunity). But as we go deeper, there are more complex emotions which if unearthed will make concluding easier.

The importance of emotion was demonstrated by an experiment conducted by a research team at the MIT Media Lab led by Alex Pentland. The team developed a sociometer, a wearable device capable of detecting interpersonal dynamics. Think of it as similar to a smartphone that picks up only the volume, pitch and pace of utterances between people having discussions without actually registering the words being spoken. Sociometer provided outputs similar to a cardiogram with various lines representing peaks and valleys. If the output of the negotiating individuals is aligned and balanced, the researchers could tell that the relationship is going well. In a controlled environment, Alex Pentland analyzed data from simulated negotiation between two people. Without hearing a single word from the negotiation and only looking at the sociometer output, he could significantly predict which pairs of people would reach an agreement. There was a positive correlation between the emotional connect of the two people and the likeliness of them coming to an agreement.

To grasp the concept of emotion in negotiation, think of the last time you negotiated with someone. What was going on in your head? You had a logical outcome in your mind, but the negotiation was being driven by emotions, like fear of failure or anxiety or positive expectation if everything went well. If you were going through emotions, the same would be the case with your counterpart. Again and again it has been conclusively proven that negotiating without analyzing the emotions involved often leads to failed outcomes. There is nothing more frustrating than the feeling that someone you are talking to isn't listening at all. There is nothing more infuriating than getting a commitment which falls apart later.

Still not convinced? Let's take an example. I give you 20 pieces of chocolate and ask you to decide how much to share with another person B. This will be a one-time decision and there would not be another chance to renegotiate. Person B's only decision would be whether to accept your offer or not. If you and person B accept the split, both of you keep the chocolates as per split. If person B does not accept the split, neither of you get any chocolate. Think for a moment before proceeding - what would be your offer to Person B?

For years, wherever I play this game with participants, I get a variety of answers. Some say they will split it 10-10, some say 5-15 and other variations in between.

One for sure, I haven't found a universal agreement between participants on what is the right split. If people were logical there would surely be one 'correct' split, right? This should be a wakeup call that logic was not what was driving the answer.

Second, the most logical outcome is offering 1 chocolate and keeping the rest for yourself. Because, logically speaking, for person B, getting 1 chocolate is better than getting no chocolate. If Person B does not accept the one chocolate offer, he would be left with no chocolate which is a worse outcome. A majority of the participants do not go for 1-19 split as it doesn't *seem fair*. Again, that is emotion usurping the rational part of the brain.

UNEARTHING UNDERLYING EMOTIONS

Piyali tried a different approach. She was a participant in our coaching sessions and wanted to test the negotiation tactics beyond her work environment. She knew that negotiation tactics work in professional settings where all parties come to the table intending to conclude. But does it work in personal settings where the counterpart does not have a specific ask in her mind? She thought she could use her active listening skills to get to know more about her mother's underlying thoughts. Possibly if she changed her strategy from persuasion to learning, she might find out more information regarding her mother's stubbornness.

Piyali started with an apology to rebuild the bridge. "I am sorry; I did not mean to bother you. It was never my intention to force you to do these."

"You don't understand. It is hard for me to do this," her mother looked up from the book she was reading.

"I know you don't like to talk about your diabetes and exercising."

"Yes, I don't like to talk about this. It is very upsetting for me."

"Upsetting for you?" Piyali mirrored in a concerned tone.

"Yes, the whole issue of diabetes is upsetting for me. I don't want to be a burden on you."

"You feel that you are a burden on me?" echoed Piyali.

"I do not want to bother you. You are very busy with your work and you are working hard to become successful in your career. I don't think it will be right to disturb you about this exercise thing."

"It seems that you are worried about asking me for help on exercising. It seems that you feel it will cause more pressure for me," Piyali resonated with the underlying emotions of her mother.

"If your father had been alive, I could have asked him for help. All these exercising, medicine timings, diet charts are confusing for me to manage. I want to do all of these, but cannot seem to get around with it. Only if your father was alive today," said her mother.

"It feels like you are lonely because father isn't here. It feels that you don't want to take my help because this might be a burden on me," resonated Piyali unearthing deeper emotions.

"Earlier, when I was young, I used to handle everything single-handedly with some help from your father. But now, I feel that I am losing track of things every day. I want to exercise or maintain diet – but it is increasingly difficult.'

"I want to help you. I sincerely want to help you."

"Are you sure?" asked her mother.

Piyali said, "Yes, sure, tell me what I can help you with."

Piyali was quite astonished at the direction this discussion had taken. Her mother felt a connection with her and was asking for her help to stick to the exercising routine. Piyali also came to see the issues from her mother's viewpoint and what it meant for her. She had no idea that her mother's superficial defiance was stemming from a much deeper baggage.

Daniel Kahneman received the 2002 Nobel Prize in Economics for his work with Amos Tversky on systematic ways the human mind deviates from rationality. His much-cited book "Thinking Fast and Slow," revolves around the dichotomy between the two modes of thought, System 1 and System 2. System 2 is our slow, rational-thinking, deliberate, analytical and consciously effortful mode of reasoning about the world. System 1, on the other hand, is our fast, automatic, intuitive and largely unconscious mode. System 1 uses association and metaphor to produce a quick and approximate presentation of reality, whereas System 2 draws on reasoned choices.

Some studies show that the human mind makes up to 35000 decisions per day. System 2 is deliberate and thus consumes a lot of energy, whereas the System 1 is fast and thus consumes a lot less energy. System 2 tires out easily. So expectedly, in a bid to save energy, more

Dig Deeper

often than not, the mind takes a shortcut and relies on System 1 thinking for an easy way out. System 2 lazily endorses what System 1 feeds to it without bothering to scrutinize if System 1 was correct at all.

For example, answer the following question: If it takes 10 machines 10 minutes to make 10 bats, how long does it take 100 machines to make 100 bats?

If your initial response was 100, that means that System 1 had jumped up to answer the problem. However, System 2 has to be triggered to really think through the right answer. The correct answer is 10 minutes. See how System 1 overpowers System 2 and is super-fast to jump to conclusions.

Where does all of this take us? Let us go back to Piyali's conversation with her mother. Initially, she was appealing to her mother's rational mind. She elaborated about the importance of exercise, cited studies made in this field and approached in a logical manner. She was appealing to her mother's System 2 thinking. And it was going no-where because her System 2 was exhausted.

As the conversation progressed, Piyali switched on her active listening mode to find out more about her mother's underlying emotions. These emotions were stopping her mother to actively seek help from Piyali and make a change in her routine. She was overwhelmed with the task of keeping everything in track. That is when Piyali started appealing to her mother's System 1 process.

Here's the surprise. Piyali's mother was hiding her feelings inside of her. She was not letting those to be surfaced. Probably even her mother would not have been aware of the intensity of these emotions or how they were affecting her. Piyali's active listening and resonating with her mother led her to feel safe enough to reveal herself. Once the emotions are on the table, it was easier for Piyali to help her mother.

Leaving your counterparts feeling arm-twisted by force or logic is the last thing you would want to do. They may not follow through on the initial agreement.

RESONATE

Resonating is about getting your counterpart to surface their inner emotions which are driving the negotiations. It is emotional intelligence. If we can let our counterpart feel safe enough to reveal himself, we might dig up more information crucial to decision making. There are 2 steps to resonate – Rehash and Acknowledge.

The first step is to rehash. To rehash is to analyze the counterpart's words and deliver it back to them in a succinct way. This, in effect, shows the counterpart that you are listening attentively. If you deliver this with a voice that radiates sincerity, you will get the counterpart to elaborate more. Rehashing lets the other person know that she has been heard and help you to clarify what you have heard.

The second step is to acknowledge the counterpart's underlying emotion – acknowledge what she is not 'saying' explicitly. Feelings crave acknowledgement. Unless feelings are acknowledged, they will cause trouble in a negotiation. But, if you acknowledge, you give the counterpart something very precious - a connection. Acknowledge does not mean you agree to what the other is saying. Acknowledge does not mean that you feel compassion for them. It just means that you grasp and recognize their emotions. It just shows that you value their point of view. It is a great way to build empathy.

Why is acknowledging their feelings important? Because tied to the expression of each feeling are some invisible questions: "Are my feelings okay?" "Do you care about them?" "Do you understand what I feel?" Verbalizing emotions and saying it aloud removes the grip that the emotion has on the brain and makes it weaker. Letting the emotion surface makes it easier for the counterpart to deal with it. Think of this as making the invisible visible. Once the emotion has been given a name,

Dig Deeper

it becomes visible – something concrete that can be dealt with. Once visible, the emotion loses its clout and relinquishes its power.

As you dig deeper into negotiations, you will realize that the reason driving a person is much different from what it was initially made out to be. People will accomplish any 'what' if they believe in the 'why'. In a negotiation, the counterpart will say 'yes' for their reasons, not yours; so it is pertinent that we can guide the counterpart to revealing their reason for the deal.

Piyali used the rehash and acknowledge tactic a few times in the discussion. "It seems that you feel that asking me for help on exercising will cause more pressure for me" or "It feels like you are lonely…"

You may wonder that the counterpart will start screaming on your face "How dare you tell me what I feel?" Here is a secret. No, that never happens. Your counterpart will not even notice. Negotiating is a taxing process. The counterpart's mind is already clouded with sentiments related to the outcome of the negotiation. Even if they are not, they will not detect that you are using the acknowledge technique to get to the emotions.

What if your analysis of the counterpart's emotion is wrong?

Yes, there is a possibility that your analysis is wrong. To avoid this, add a softening phrase "It seems like", "It feels like", "It looks like" and so on before the rehashed statement. In case your analysis is wrong and the counterpart says "No, I don't feel like that" you can get away by saying that it felt like that to you. And then the counterpart may proceed to reveal their actual feeling.

Examples of Rehash and Acknowledge:

- "It seems like you have heard negative feedback about the products that we sell."
- "It feels like you had a tiring day."

- "It sounds like you have spoken to existing customers before giving us an appointment."
- "It looks like you are excited about taking this job."

Car buying is an area of great interest for negotiators. These are high-value purchases with wide margins and lots of fluctuations between emotion and logic. I recollect an incident when I visited a local Tata Motors Showroom for purchasing a car accessory. While I was waiting for the accessory to be brought from a nearby storage warehouse, a man came in to buy a new car.

He seemed to be from an affluent family and was looking for an additional car for family use, mostly a mid-range hatchback. After about forty-five minutes of inspecting the different variants and features, he finalized on a model variant and told the salesman "We need this in blue."

The salesman said, "Ok Sir, let me check with my inventory."

He pulled up the inventory, "Sir, blue is not available now. However, if you do a booking now, we can arrange for delivery with 30 days."

"That's a lot of time. I cannot wait for that long."

"Sir, we have silver ready with us. You can get it in 3 days."

"No, I want in blue."

"Sir, silver is one of the bestselling models. Silver is the easiest to maintain and does not show scratches easily. The car body under the silver paint is greyish in colour and hence scratches are not much visible. This colour also hides dirt effectively and so you need not wash frequently. You can do with one or two washes a month," he tried to convince the client. He knew that if the client walks away, it will be impossible to bring him back to the showroom again. The sale might go to a rival dealer or competitor brand.

"No, I want the blue model. How early can you deliver?"

"Sir, our system shows 30 days. But, I can check with my seniors and maybe bring down the delivery to 25 days."

"No, that is too long."

"Sir, as you are looking for a quick delivery, I would still request you to consider the Silver colour. Silver also has a great resale value, in fact, the highest for this model. Plus, it is a low maintenance colour. This would be the right colour for you."

"We will take the blue colour only," and he proceeded to get up and walk away.

The salesman was dejected. He had lost the client. As he was walking the client to the door, he said, "Sir, it seems that you feel strongly about the colour of the car you are going to purchase."

"Yes, the colour of the car is important for my wife. She is very particular about getting a blue one. Our house has blue highlights. She wants something that matches."

That was a bombshell moment. The salesperson then managed to get the customer back into the showroom and sold a more expensive model with an available blue variant.

Only if he had led with rehash and acknowledge tactic, it would have saved him time and headache.

HOW TO RESONATE WITH REHASH AND ACKNOWLEDGE

5 step guide to rehash and acknowledge method:

1. Start with a sincere tone
2. Seek to understand the emotion behind the counterpart's asks.
3. Rehash and acknowledge their underlying feelings. Use softening phrases like "It seems…" / "It feels like…" / "It sounds like…" / "It looks like…"

4. Silence. Let the counterpart evaluate the rehash.
5. Do this over and over till you are clear of the underlying reasons.

KEEP YOUR EMOTIONS IN CHECK

In November 2016, Richard Keedwell, a retired British engineer, was accused of driving at a speed of 36mph in a 30mph zone when he was out for Christmas shopping in Worcester along with his wife. He got a speeding ticket in his mail for £100.

He was convinced that it was not the case. He spent about two and a half years attending several court appearances to fight the issue. After asking for evidence from the Police, he hired an expert in radar and electronics, Tim Farrow, who said that he may have been mistakenly accused because of the "double doppler" effect. This happens when the camera's radar measuring the speed of a vehicle accidentally bounces off a second vehicle traveling in the same direction and thus incorrectly captures the speed.

Convinced with the logic, Richard hired barristers to fight a legal battle in court. He spent about £21000 in appealing up to the last hearing in August 2019, plus £7000 approximately on court costs plus travel expenses.

Instead of settling the £100 fine, he spent close to £30000 in a protracted legal battle to prove his point. Needless to say, he finally lost and was asked to pay for the court costs and other fines.

A strong message this example brings to the table is knowing your emotions before coming to the table. While you are looking to unearth emotions of the counterpart, knowing your own emotions is of crucial importance. Extremely strong emotions will cloud judgement and get you to lose track of objectives. The need to prove your arguments at any cost may be disastrous even when the evidences were pointing otherwise.

ACKNOWLEDGING GOES A LONG WAY

One of my ex-bosses was a marvelous negotiator. We were on our way to meet a client in Mumbai. It was cold December. The meeting was scheduled at 10 AM, so we took an early morning flight. It was an urgent meeting that had to be done. The client was going on holidays from next week and the deal had to be finalized before that. Else, we stood to lose out a good 3 weeks to get the deal back on track. So, we found the first flight to Mumbai and the first hotel who would take a booking on such short notice.

We reached the hotel where we had booked for the day. The hotel had a check-in time at 12 noon. We had reached at 8 AM and were looking to freshen up before meeting the client. It was a deal worth lakhs, so we didn't want to take any chances. If you end up in a crumpled smelling shirt in front of a client, you do not really put up a great impression. Being properly groomed is the first that they teach in sales.

How do we get a check-in 4 hours before the scheduled time?

When we had arrived at the hotel, we found quite a few guests crowding at the reception clearing their bills. So, waiting for the queue to clear, we were strolling around the main lobby when we overhead guests who had just checked-out saying that they had a fabulous event last night. We struck up a conversation with one of them and came to know that a large company had thrown a party last evening and guests were checking in and out throughout the night.

This was a clue that my ex-boss wanted to use. He was good at identifying people's underlying emotions and how to get around them. Directly approaching the front desk will not really solve the problem. The front desk is trained to keep such requests at bay. They would probably ask us to keep the luggage with the concierge and come back later. So, he devised a master plan. He knew that the hotel's staff changed shifts around 8:30 AM. He approached the front desk with a big smile.

"Hi, how are you doing?"

"Welcome Sir," the lady at the front desk smiled back.

"There seems to be a lot of guests at such an early hour."

"Yes, we have many guests checking out today morning," she replied.

"Many guests checking out?"

"Yes, we usually have numerous early-morning checkouts when there are large gatherings for events. Last evening was one of them. Managing timely check-outs is critical as guests have flights to catch."

"Oh! It looks like you had a tiring shift," he said acknowledging the underlying feeling.

"Yes. Really tiring day today. We had guests checking in and checking out all night."

"All night?" mirrored my ex-boss.

The front desk staff explained how a large company had scheduled an event for five hundred customers last night and it was chaotic for everyone in the hotel including the front desk who were coordinating for the guests. From handling room service to coordinating for luggage, the front desk had a tough night.

"It feels like it was a hectic night at the front desk," he rehashed and acknowledged the underlying emotion.

"Yes. Many of the guests have been checking out till early hours today morning. It was quite a rush but ended well. We have only a few more guests to attend to from this event."

They chatted for a while about the service industry in general and how frantic it becomes when there are large gatherings for hotels like this. Having resonated with the front desk staff, he finally placed his request. "Well, it seems that you had handled the guests quite well. We are also here to meet a client of ours. It was an urgent meeting and had to take the early morning flight. You were saying that some of the customers might have checked out early, so will it be possible to get us an early check-in. I do not mean to push you; we are only looking to freshen up before going to the meeting."

And he paused. He let that sink in. He maintained the smile and the sincerity of the request.

She looked up from her computer and glanced at him. Then she stared back hard into the computer.

"Let me see what I can do." And in some time, she proceeded to give us two rooms with early check-in at no additional costs.

Next time dealing with customer service or front desk, show your humane side and you will get what you ask for. This also works like charm if you are trying to schedule an appointment with a senior company executive and have to push his secretary to get the best slot. Dump all formal emails or pleading. Appeal to their emotional side and you will be surprised how quickly you get the appointment.

ANCHOR THE EMOTIONS

Negotiations will often get you into territories where you have to convince your counterpart to consider propositions which may not be fully in their favor. Or cases where you have to press forward an option which is contrary to their viewpoint. In such cases, the first thing that your counterpart is going to do is negate whatever you have said or get into a flurry of anger and resentment. If not addressed methodically, these may turn into blame games.

Have you heard of the phrase "I do not mean to hurt you…" or "I don't want to sound exaggerating…" and then the person proceeded to do just the same? This technique is used most effectively in cases where you can be confronted or when there is a conflict that you are trying to resolve. These are difficult conversations where you need to knock out the pessimism sooner to get the ball rolling. To diffuse the negative, you have to proactively attack all or most of the negatives even before they are spoken. You are practically reaching into someone's head and shutting out the negatives even before they can levy these blames on you.

I use this technique often when I pitch something to my network. If I would like them to contribute or share their time for a cause, I start with "You would probably think I am taking too much liberty of my friendship with you for this request. We are coming up with ..." What this does is address what the other person might feel and takes it out. More often than not, I get the response, "No worries, let me see what best I can do."

CHAPTER SUMMARY

Getting a commitment is easy provided you know how to approach the counterpart. Human beings have two systems of thinking – System 1 which is irrational and instinctive and System 2 which is deliberate and rational. System 1 is quick to act and uses less energy whereas System 2 is slow and uses more energy. The human brain switches over to System 1 thinking wherever possible. For a negotiator, this is a gold mine. If we can influence the counterpart's System 1 thinking, it could lead to quicker rapport building and connection. Here are some key takeaways from this chapter:

- Empathy is a crucial element in negotiation. Both you and your counterpart can come to the discussion with opposing views and demands. But the counterpart should always feel that you are empathetic to their stances. Empathy does not require you to agree with what they are saying. Empathy is stepping into their shoes and understanding their emotions/pain.
- The quickest way to build empathy is to resonate with your counterpart. Use the Rehash and Acknowledge technique.

- To rehash, paraphrase what the counterpart is saying in your own words and relay it back to them in a succinct manner. It shows that you are listening attentively and gets your counterpart to elaborate more.

- The next step is to acknowledge the counterpart's underlying emotion. This may require a bit of dexterity and emotional intelligence. Use a softening phrase "it seems like/ It feels like / It sounds like / It looks like" with the acknowledgement. Feelings crave acknowledgement. If you acknowledge the feelings of your counterpart, you build a strong connection.

- Use a sincere and composed tone. After rehash and acknowledge is done, pause for a few seconds for its effect to take place.

- Acknowledging the negative emotions goes a long way in diffusing the negatives. If someone is having strong negative feelings about you or what you are about to say can create a negative feeling, acknowledge them upfront. It diffuses the negative very quickly and makes the counterpart more open to what you have to say next.

NO IS MUSIC

In the initial years of my career, I learned a very valuable lesson.

We used to do a lot of calls trying to get prospective customers to buy courses from our academy. I recall not one but uncountable experience during those initial years when we used to get stood up. Here is how it used to proceed. And, probably it does for many of you who are reading this book.

We get on a call with the customer, "Sir, my name is Abhishek Datta. Is this a good time to talk to you?"

Customer: "Yes?"

"Sir, we have different courses which you, your spouse or your children can avail. These are classroom-based courses with hands-on teaching, where we give you in-depth knowledge and practical training. Would you like to know about the courses?"

Customer: "Yes. What course do you have?"

We would then proceed to outline the various courses that we

NO is Music

offered and what the customer can learn from them. We would provide the customer with the class timings, batch structure, curriculum, market opportunities after the course, and other additional features that we provided.

Customer: "That's great. I was searching for something like this for my daughter. Do you have a brochure?"

"Yes Sir, can you share your email ID? I will share the details. Would you want to know anything else about the courses?"

"Yes, can you send me the course fees structure and payment terms."

"Sure Sir, I am sending it right away."

And, we used to feel very happy with the way it went. Perfect. Just perfect. What a flow! Everything fell into place during the call. Smoothly done. We would get pumped up and go get a coffee as a reward.

Two days later, we would follow up with an email to the client, "Sir, which course do you think will suit you?"

No response. Probably, he was busy with work.

Fourth day, we would call him up, "Sir, I had emailed you. Did you get a chance to look into the email?"

"Err, No, let me check it and get back to you."

"Ok Sir, do you want any more information on the courses?"

"Yes, do you offer any discounts? I am sure you do. Can you tell me what discount can I get on these?"

We would hold the phone for a moment and say, "Sir, we can do a 10% discount for you."

Customer: "Thanks. I will inform you by tomorrow."

"We are looking forward to a positive response."

Next day goes. No response from the customer. We follow-up via calls and email. No response. Finally, after following up for another few days, we give up on this lead and focus on another one.

All too familiar? I bet, as people in sales are prone to do, our over-optimism drags us on this path over and over again lead after lead. What is wrong with this call? Everything. Yes, everything is wrong with this call.

The prospective customer knows this, instinctively. All the initial agreements to our questions, eagerness to know in detail and the keenness to start the course is just an excuse to get more information. When we get the first few 'yeses', our adrenaline starts pumping with enthusiasm, we feel excited that finally we are on our way to get what we want. We start feeling good, positive feelings hijack the brain and before we know, we have lost our power in the negotiation. He has all the information he needs; he is least bothered to come back to the negotiating table. He is now calling the shots. The counterpart can now arm-twist us into anything that he wants. We have lost the game.

That is what we, as negotiators, call a fake 'yes'. A fake 'yes' is a yes which is used to get more information and objectively ends in a 'no'. A fake 'yes' hides deeper objections.

NO IS GOLD

If 'Yes' is not the correct way to go, what is the other option? 'No' – you guessed it right. After multiple failed calls with prospective customers, I started on my journey to get the customer to say 'No'. Beware that in-between 'Yes' and 'No' is 'Maybe' which is equally or even more dangerous than 'yes'.

'Yes' is phony. 'No' is gold. But before we go there, let's discuss 'Maybe'. 'Maybe' does not serve any purpose. 'Maybe' muddles the water. With a 'Maybe', neither party has any clue to where the other person stands. When you hear a 'Maybe', you don't know what it means. It is a way of meaning different things to different parties.

If you are optimistic, you would infer 'Maybe' to be a 'yes'. Did he say 'yes'? Did he just agree to what I offered? He just needs a little bit of push to a full yes. If you are not sure about the deal, you would infer 'Maybe' as a 'no'. Did he disagree? Or, does he not know fully and are looking for more guidance? 'Maybe' is keeping you hanging with a noose around your neck with all the emotions and doubts. Long enough it will kill the deal. So, as a trained negotiator, you have to get past the 'maybe' phase as quickly as possible. If your counterpart is sticking to 'Maybe', there is a bigger issue there. Start digging deeper. Children are taught to respect each other's feelings. For some, 'Maybe' is a subtle way of saying 'No' but sparing the counterpart a bad feeling. It is a way to avoid a conflict.

I remember a colleague of mine who always used to say 'maybe' whenever we used to ask him to join us for an after-office party. And never once did he join a party. After we learned it the hard way, we stopped asking him to come with us.

With 'Yes' and 'Maybe' out of the way, let's focus on 'no'. Why is 'no' such a powerful word? To answer this, let's go through a scenario. If you are working and you ask your boss for a leave, what is the first thing she says? "No." If you are a manager, and an employee comes up asking for leave, what is the first thing that you say or crosses your mind? "No." And after that, the next response is "Why do you want a leave?" If you are a parent and your child comes asking you for ice-cream, what is the first word you say? "No" and then you ask why he wants that.

'No' gives a sense of power, a sense of control over the situation. 'No' protects. 'No' ensures we feel in charge. Like it is for us, the same applies to the counterpart. If it is your counterpart saying "No", then he feels in control and safeguarded, his nerves calm down and he is now more open to hearing your side of the story. A good negotiator always strives to ensure that the counterpart feels in control, even though you are playing the cards. A good negotiator strives to get his counterpart to say 'No' during the initial course of the discussions.

From our perspective, hearing 'No' is quite difficult. Our alarm systems start beeping. Our faces go red. All hell breaks loose. We feel violated. Our sense of self-worth is hit. And this is a natural reaction when we hear 'No'. As negotiators, we have to overcome our inner urge to react to a 'No' and take 'No' just at face value. It is an opportunity to discover more about the counterpart and get him to open up. Change your interpretation of 'no' to mean an invitation to dig deeper into the counterpart's world.

GETTING MORE RESOURCES FOR THE TEAM

Rahul, a friend of mine from school, was the team lead for an automation project at Simple IT Exchange. They were working on an AI-based email marketing and tracking tool for a foreign client. He started with a 10-member team of developers. But about three months into the project, they got rightsized to a 6-member team as the client was not willing to pump in more money. It was a pilot project that they had taken up for the client at a nominal cost in expectation of getting more projects later on. That was mistake number one. But, we have already discussed similar instances earlier in the book. The side effect of picking up a low margin or zero margin project is that there is no room for maneuvers. A small change here and there, a squeeze by the client or an extra ask can lead to suffocation. Same had happened here.

Rahul was sympathetic to the situation and had agreed to release 4 developers to other projects. He now had 6 developers on his team. And all 6 were working overtime. His main objective was to get over with the project as quickly as possible and prevent any cost overruns. He would require another 2 months if everything went as planned.

But, nothing goes as planned. One morning, he got called into his manager's cabin.

NO is Music

"Listen Rahul. I will be blunt. We are losing money on this project. We have to get over the project as quickly as possible."

Rahul expected this, "Sir, we understand the situation. We are on it. We will be able to deliver on sharp two months."

"That is too much. And I have another bad news for you."

Rahul felt that tightening in his guts. Another bad news.

"Rahul, we have got a new contract from another client and I need to cut another 2 developers from your team. Our current project is a loss-making one and we need to move resources to this new project and recover some of the cost."

Rahul was not expecting so hard a shock. A further two-person cut means that the project will not get delivered on time; or the quality of deliverables will degrade massively. And that would cost them the client or tarnish the company's reputation. He was in two minds on how to tackle the issue. If he provided a straight forward logic, that wouldn't suffice. His boss had already put a lot of thought into it. If he let the project fail, then his reputation will also be tainted. He had to find a way to get his boss see the reality. He had to get him to the core of the issue. Then, he delivered one of the hard-hitting 'no' questions I have ever heard.

"Sir, do you want the project to fail?"

"No," his manager almost screamed and paused.

Rahul waited for a few seconds and continued, "Sir, this is a pilot project and if we can deliver to the client's satisfaction, we can get larger projects which will recover our costs. It is our reputation and future cash flow at stake. It seems you are in a tight spot on budgets, but if you can help me here, we can really make a difference to the client."

Long silence. Then his manager said, "You can keep all six developers. But get the project completed in two months without fail."

Rahul just prevented a disaster from happening.

'No' when used in negotiation gets the counterpart to think and see more clearly. With falsities and feigning off the agenda, the counterpart can now see things in black and white. It helps to clear out any fuzziness around the item being negotiated and cuts straight to the heart of the issue.

MORE NO-ORIENTED QUESTIONS

1. When wooing your customer away from a competitor – "Are you better off than you were before using this product?"
2. When a politician is asking for votes – "Is there less unemployment in the country than there was few years ago?"
3. When trying to get through on a cold call – "Is this a bad time to talk?"
4. When asking a very senior and reputed person for their time – "Is it a horrible idea to spare 5 minutes to listen to this request?"
5. When pitching about the benefits of the product – "Do you want to lose out on a potential revenue of INR 10 Lakhs?"
6. When comparing your product with competitors – "Does the competitor's product give you X, Y, Z?"
7. When asking for a holiday from your boss – "Would it be dangerously bad if I take 2 days off next week?"
8. When trying to find out what is blocking the counterpart – "Do you disagree with this?" [The counterpart usually replies with "No, I don't disagree but here are somethings we need to clear" and gives you the objections.]
9. When negotiating with the vendor – "Do you want to lose out on this opportunity to associate with such a large brand?"
10. When you want someone to respond to your emails/requests/

NO is Music

phone calls – "Have you given up on …?"

11. When you want to ask a question to someone – "Would it be embarrassing to ask you a question?"

LEARN TO LOVE NO IN SALES

One of the biggest fears for people in sales is hearing customers say "No". So, people gun for a 'yes' answer in every step of the sales process. However, the first training I impart when coaching is to go for a 'No' early on in the conversation. Don't get me wrong. 'Yes' is the final aim in a sales process. But it should start with 'No' early on and then move to a final true 'yes'. Not the phony fake 'yes' we spoke earlier; but a real commitment to the deal. That will happen only when all objections are cleared from the table.

There are two 'Nos' in sales – the generic 'no' and the objection 'no'.

In the early stage of a sales process, the 'No' that you will hear is mostly the generic 'No' and these are often less substantial than the Objection 'No'. You have to manage these Generic 'Nos' differently.

When a prospect says he doesn't have time, or the product is expensive or the company is not interested, they are not saying 'no' to your product or offering. At this juncture, the prospect does not have enough information to possibly conclude that your offering is of no interest to him. What they are guarding is their time, attention and credibility. You haven't give them a compelling reason to hear you out.

Think of when a salesperson was pushing you to say 'yes', your first response was 'No'. People, in general, instinctively put up hurdles when they feel like they're being sold to. So, when we are trying to sell, why not give the prospect the full liberty to say the generic 'no' at the outset! Make people feel okay saying 'No' to you.

What I have seen in my career is that when somebody is given the liberty to say 'No', the person takes notice. He wakes up and really consider the proposal. We force him to think twice before answering. For prospect calls, we recommend starting the call in this fashion inviting the client to say 'No' in the first step.

"Sir, I am calling you from XYZ. We are manufacturers of ABC products and I am giving you a call you to see if you require such products for your company. I don't know if we are a fit, so, if you say No, we will end the call. However, if you feel that we can add value, then…"

This works on the basic premise of loss aversion. Most people are loss averse, they can go to lengths to avoid losses. When we are asking them for 'No', their loss aversion mindset kicks in. They feel that if they say 'No', the might lose out on something without even knowing it. Most will give you a patient hearing or give you an alternate time to call when they can spare time to hear you out.

The only case you hear 'No' to the above call is when they do not have anything to do with your product. In that case, you are better off scrapping the prospect than going ahead and wasting your time.

The objection 'No' is much deeper than the generic 'No'. The objection 'No' is when your prospect considers the proposal and then says 'No'. For example, they do not have a budget for the product.

This is a smokescreen that the client has put up – an objection 'No' which hides information. These objections aren't fixed. It is not the work of a salesperson to overcome Objection 'Nos' – it is the prospect's work. Your job, as a salesperson, is to guide the prospect to that conclusion.

You can respond to budget questions like:

"Sir, I have not been able to demonstrate the ROI on the product. If we can demonstrate fast ROI when our product is deployed, is this something that you may be interested in talking about?"

Or you can flip the question (using techniques shared earlier), "It seems that with the current economic situation, many companies are under financial pressure. If for a moment we think that budget is not a concern, then would you still not be interested in going through the ROI details for this product?"

This is where listening and resonating techniques will help draw more information from the prospect. Find the root cause.

In some cases, 'no' can mean no. The prospect does not need the product or service. When you dig deeper, and get a feel of the undercurrent driving the decisions, you may discover reasons for the sale not closing are genuine and neither you nor the prospect can do anything about it. It is best, then, to leave the prospect and not push anymore.

RECRUITING WITH NO.

There is a saying "Hire for attitude" and it is specifically true for fresher candidates or those without much work experience. How do you test attitude in a candidate and if she is the right fit for your company?

Go ahead and dissuade her from joining your company.

"The work here entails a lot of overtime and weekend work. You wouldn't be able to cope up with the pressure, right?"

"You have to travel a long distance to get to the office. That will be a big daily headache for you. I think you shouldn't join the company."

See the response that you get. Is it attuned to the values of your company, or are they self-serving? Is she able to overcome personal inhibitions? Most candidates answer these questions with "No Sir, I will be able to work for your company as …" and they proceed to give the reason behind their conviction.

Keep experimenting with this technique – it works like charm.

'No' has a lot of advantages.

- 'No' cuts to the core of the issue. It ensures both parties focus on the real issue at hand.

- 'No' prevents both parties from making the wrong decision. It brings more clarity in their thinking process.
- 'No' gives the counterpart the feeling of control; it makes them feel important, secure and safe.
- 'No' is the quickest way to avoid wasting time in wrong negotiations.
- 'No' empowers.

HOW TO HIKE A CONTRACT VALUE?

Suman was an upcoming interior designer. He was in the market for about 5 years and had done some good quality interiors for small clients. He worked across smaller cities and towns in Eastern India. With a strong command over design skills and the contractor market, he was growing fast. However, most of his work was low budget and more run off the mill. He was aiming for larger clients from the metros where there would be a significant profit margin to work with. But he was unable to convert them. The margins were squeezed so low that he did not find the inclination to pick up the project. He would grudgingly tell the prospects that he will work on a budget and then never return to them again. I met him when he was a participant in one of our coaching sessions where he wanted to upgrade his negotiation skills.

He recollected an incident of how he used 'No' to seal his first large deal with a client from Kolkata. This particular prospect was a known industrialist from Kolkata with different properties across the city. He wanted to engage Suman as an Interior Designer for one of his smaller properties to start with. It was a 3BHK flat and the entire interior had to be worked on right from flooring to woodwork to colour.

After a preliminary discussion, Suman quoted him a budget of INR 16 Lakhs. If you have experience in interior design you would know that a quote of INR 16 Lakhs is on the lower side. The industrialist had years of experience in bargaining deals for his business and loved to play hardball. INR 16 Lakhs was a very reasonable price for him to afford. However, given his inclination to bargain for deals, he called Suman to his office.

"Hi Suman, I got your proposal. You have done a good job in outlining the work details. However, the amount quoted is on the higher side. If you can complete the project in INR 10 Lakhs, I can sign the agreement right away."

Suman was not expecting such a low offer. He got anchored immediately (a technique which we will learn later) and proposed an amount of INR 14 Lakhs. This is a big mistake which he should not have done. Never give off a number so easily.

Seeing Suman reducing the quote, the prospect came up with a counter-offer to break Suman to his limits. "See, the budget that I have is only INR 10 Lakhs, but because I like what you have provided in the project outline, I will try to increase it to INR 11 lakhs. But nothing more than that."

Suman was frustrated. He could not let this happen. In fact, at INR 14 Lakhs, he had already forgone a major portion of his margin. He felt he should just give up and never return to the prospect again. But, he gave one last try.

"Sir, it seems that you have a financial constraint and you want to get the project done in a low budget. However, there is a cost associated with experienced workmen. The labour market is undergoing huge shifts and the best workmen are moving out of the state for better-paying projects. We have a stronghold with few contractors who provide experienced workmen in projects such as these. But a low budget is a real hindrance and at this price point, we would be able to afford only the semi-skilled workmen. Would you like to get a finished home for yourself that will start deteriorating in a year's time?"

Oh! What an empathy-building counter. Suman summarized the issues he was facing with a slight nudge that he might have to reduce the work quality if the budget is reduced. He played on the word "home" to make it more personal for the prospect. Finally, he ended with a powerful 'No' question.

The prospect paused to rethink.

"I will be gifting this flat to my daughter to stay and study. It is near to her college and will be easier to commute. After her college days are over, we can use the place as a weekend get-away. We are looking for something which can last for a reasonable time. What can you do to make it better?"

"The initial budget was INR 16 lakhs. That covers the cost for the latest designs, quality materials, and the best workmen. If you have researched, you would know that what I offered is a very competitive rate. Since this is a one-time investment, I would like to show you some more designs. If you like want a better finish on the modular kitchen with German Laminates and design changes to the woodwork," he pulled out some more design variations, "it would cost another approx. INR 3 Lakhs, but will give a considerably distinct premium look."

After more design iterations, Suman sealed the deal at INR 17 Lakhs. Last time I heard, he was tasked with refurbishing another two of the prospect's homes.

'No' is like an electric saw. You don't need brute force to cut with an electric saw. You just have to guide the blade to the right place. The saw will do the work for itself.

DEALING WITH ULTIMATUMS

How do you react when someone gives you an ultimatum – a take it or leave it scenario.

"If you back out now, we will blacklist you and you won't find any work again with us."

"You don't want to take this to court, do you? Then accept what is getting offered here."

"That's our final offer. Take it or leave it."

"We can never do that."

When I was working out of Mumbai in 2011, I met Biren, a 40-something guy, who dealt with off-the-shelf software for accounting and productivity suites. Off-the-shelf software is ready-to-use software produced for the mass market and which can be deployed immediately. He used to procure in bulk and sell them to various small and medium businesses across the city. His friend had recently introduced him to a reputed company which developed antivirus and security software and asked if he might be interested in the deal. Since the customer base was the same and he would have to spend very little additional resources to market the new software, he readily agreed.

Over the next few weeks, he met the company manager to negotiate the deal and both sides agreed to go ahead. But, before the signing can happen, Biren met an industry expert in a networking event who informed him that the pricing was much higher than what the company generally offered to other channel partners.

Biren was upset and emailed the company with the new-found information and asked for a revision of the price.

The manager was furious and called back. "We cannot change the price. We have been negotiating on this deal for weeks and we had agreed to all the pricing terms. Now, we will not change the price. Take it or leave it."

Biren, a seasoned negotiator, knew the first rule to any ultimatums. Ignore the ultimatum. Ultimatum is often a spontaneous emotional reaction when the counterpart feels violated, frustrated or has to save face in his company. The worst thing for Biren to do would have been focusing on the ultimatum and make it more difficult for the manager to back away from his statement later in the negotiation process. More often than not, in business relationships such as these, the counterpart does not know how things may play out in the next few days, weeks, months or years. Things might change or improve. The manager might change in the company. Pricing in general can shift. Other terms can be worked out. And hence, the best way to deal with an ultimatum is to ignore it and go past it. Make no mention of the alleged threat.

Biren started, "It seems that you are frustrated regarding the last-minute hiccups. Both of us have been working towards closing the deal for some time now. We both know that a deal can be made, just that we are unable to find a common solution. I would suggest that we keep working to find out more about how things can be worked out." Biren ignored the ultimatum or the 'take it or leave it' statement.

The second rule is to offset any further negatives from the counterpart's side. Biren knew that the manager can drag the deal and make it difficult for him. He had to diffuse any other negatives that the manager might come up with. He may have already told his boss regarding the pricing and any last-minute change will damage his reputation.

Biren continued, "We understand that these last-minute hiccups may delay the deal further and take up more time. This may also be frustrating at your end convincing others in your organizations of these changes, however reasonable they may be, given the prevalent market pricing. However, we would like to continue to work with you to make the deal happen." He acknowledged the underlying dynamics and any emotional nuances if he had to go back to his boss for a price renege.

Third, let them know that the threat or the ultimatum is not credible. If the threat is just a negotiating tactic, all the more reason to call it out. If the threat is an actual ultimatum, no harm in trying one more time appealing to their interests.

Biren continued, "Yours is one of the most reputed companies in security software. If you look at the market data, you can see for yourself that the pricing can be worked out to a rate lower than quoted. Having worked with you for the past few weeks, it is in both of our interests that we do not want the deal to fall through at this juncture over one issue. So, let us work on resolving the hindrances in a way that is agreeable to both of us." He appealed to the manager to check the market data and calibrate the pricing.

The manager came back in two days with revised pricing consistent with prevailing market rates. Biren sealed the deal. Most ultimatums are not true deal breakers. People feel violated or frustrated or need to show control or save face or gain some tactical advantage. In which case, ignoring the ultimatum is the best possible path.

When should you give an ultimatum?

You should give an ultimatum only if this is really an ultimatum – something that you will follow through and not go back. But, if you are trying to mount a pressure tactic, better not to go ahead with an ultimatum. Soften it and give the counterpart reasons why the deal cannot be done under the current terms.

DON'T LET A NEGOTIATION END IN A NO

This chapter ends with a strong but powerful philosophy. Never end a negotiation with a 'no'. A negotiation should and always end in either a 'Yes' or an understanding the why behind the 'No'. This is true for both parties. Have you heard of people who come out of a negotiation saying, "I don't even know what went wrong there" or "Is that person crazy not to accept such a good deal?" That is the feeling we want to avoid here.

If both parties do not agree to the deal, each side must communicate why the deal fell through. It can be a simple explanation of which terms could not be agreed upon. You may discover that the other side has needs that you cannot meet or that your competitor can create value that you simply cannot. A good way to end is to ask the question: "What would it have taken for us to reach an agreement?" And you may discover options that you had overlooked, needs that you hadn't taken into consideration or issues that you did not explore in-depth. Even if there was no mutually agreeable solution, you will come to know what your competitors may be offering and how you can up the game next time.

In business and in life, we would be negotiating with the same party multiple times over and over again. We never know when conditions can become favorable again for the deal or when either party is in critical need of what the other offers. In that case, it should be clear that if the terms could be renegotiated or looked at, the deal can be discussed again.

CHAPTER SUMMARY

If there is one thing that can revolutionize the way we negotiate it is the power of 'No'. 'No' is the least used and most wrongly understood word in negotiation. Many often approach the negotiation process with the intension to keep the counterpart saying 'yes' at all steps. This 'Yes' approach can backfire as the counterpart can feel cornered to say something that he doesn't fully agree with and often leads to reversal or backtracking after the deal has been agreed to.

Here are the key takeaways from this chapter:

- 'Yes' is phony. 'Yes' said at the early stage of the negotiation are often useless and does not contribute anything to the negotiation. Contrary to popular strategies, initial 'Yeses' harm the negotiation by hiding the real motivations and pain points of the counterpart.

- 'Maybe' is worse. 'Maybe' does not serve any purpose. It means different things to different people. If you are optimistic, you will interpret 'Maybe' as a possible 'yes'. If you aren't, then you would

NO is Music

interpret 'Maybe' as a possible 'no'. It just leaves you hanging.

- 'No' is gold. 'No' serves two purposes: One, it gives a sense of power to your counterpart making them feel superior and safeguarded. It is like an ego massage. Once they feel safeguarded, they are more open to lower their guards. Two, 'No' gets the counterpart to correct us and hence reveal more of what they feel is right.

- Hearing a 'No' may be difficult for you. You have to suppress your initial urge to react to the word and take the words as it is. Just a 'No'. Learn to appreciate 'no' as a way of uncovering objections in the deal and probing the counterpart with more questions. In sales, welcoming 'No' in the initial phases lets you build your pitch around those objections and guards you against a potential pull out at the last moment.

- Ultimatums are "take it or leave it" statements. They are emotional reactions from the counterpart and more often than not empty threats. As a negotiator, ignore ultimatums. Do not react to them but skirt around them and continue with your point. Never respond to ultimatum either directly or indirectly. Offset the negatives that may come up because of the ultimatum. If the ultimatums are not credible let the counterpart know.

- All negotiations must end with either a 'Yes' or an understanding the why behind the 'No'. Either both you and the counterpart agree to the deal or both of you know why the deal couldn't take place in the first place.

FOCUS QUESTIONS

About 6 months after Suman's incident, one Saturday, we got a customer walking into our office. She was about 35 years of age and was accompanied by her husband and a kid of 6 years. Nothing out of ordinary. Prospects regularly enquire with us and see if our offerings were in line with their requirements.

She introduced herself as Rekha Mazoomdar. The name rang a bell. I had heard the name somewhere. I tried to recollect. While she was waiting in the customer area, I looked up on the internet. And yes, I was right. She was a well-known journalist who was active in reporting for a popular Indian News Channel. I haven't seen her off-late, but I remember her vivid style of reporting, dashing across the country and going to the heart of the hottest news in India. She used to cover ground-breaking political and socio-economic news in her super energetic panache putting herself in the path to get maximum for her story. She was vivacious and spirited the last time I saw on television.

I glanced back at her. Yes, she looked familiar now. Age was starting to show but she still had the tingling resemblance of her on-screen personality. I called her and her family to my cabin.

"Hi, my name is Abhishek Datta," extending my hand for a shake.

"Hi, I am Rekha Mazoomdar and I was looking to know more about the Jewellery Making Course that you have."

"Are you the same Rekha Mazoomdar, the journalist who covered some of the biggest television breaking news in India?"

"Yes," she shied with a strained smile, "but I am not a journalist anymore. I quit my job 7-8 years back after my first child." She glanced at her kid running her fingers through his hair.

"Okay." Her tone had a touch of dejection, but we proceed to go on, "How can I assist you today?"

"Like I said, I wanted to know more about the course details. I want to learn something new."

"Learn something new?" I mirrored.

"Yes, I want to learn something new. I have free time on my hand and want to explore my creative side. I have done basic art and crafts work when I was in school, but since then, I haven't really used my hands for creative work. My kid is also grown up and I do not have to look after him continuously," she explained.

"So, it seems that you want to use your free time to learn some hands-on work and revisit your creative trait," I rehashed.

"Yes, right."

"Great. What if you can convert your creativity into a business?" I asked.

"That would be interesting. I have never been into business. It is a new area for me. But it sure sounds interesting. Do I require some special skills to be in business? I used to be a journalist, but I have lost that touch now. Can I do something like that from home?" she asked.

"No and Yes. No, you don't require any special skills to be in business. And yes, you can do from home." I explained to her about business in general and how she can start from home with minimal investment.

"How much money are you looking to earn monthly?" I asked.

"I don't have a particular number in mind. I used to draw a decent salary when I was a journalist. But that is past." Her tone again shadowed by sensed a wave of dejection. "I guess I can start this as a hobby and then build into a business."

There was something she was trying to hold back. Not consciously, but something which can have a significant impact on the outcome. Something that uncovered may relive her and benefit us in the process.

"It feels like you are missing some of your old days as a journalist. It seems you enjoyed those days. How can I help to make today better?" I acknowledged her feelings and paused to let the question sink in.

She inhaled deeply and looked at her husband. "Since I had the child, I had given up on my journalist career. And with that I have given up thinking about myself. My entire focus for the past 7-8 years has been in nurturing my family and taking care of them. Not even once have I thought about restarting my career." Her eyes moistened around the corners. "It has been difficult for me to keep my inner feelings suppressed. It is not that my husband has ever said 'No' to anything I do, but I want to do something now. Something on my own." She shifted her gaze towards the floor and held still for few seconds.

"It sounds like you want to become self-independent," I rehashed and acknowledged her.

"That is right. I want to become self-independent. I want to re-ignite my career, albeit in a different field. I want to become independent."

We were almost there. "What about self-independence is important to you?"

"I need my own identity," she declared with a bright glowing face. Gone was the dejection in her voice. The twinkle in her eyes was back. She was now ready to listen to what we can offer to help her develop her identity. She registered for a course that helped her learn professional creative skills and start a small business from home. We helped her with setting up a complete business from procurement to sales to delivery. She now employees five women and together they manufacture and supply their products across the country.

How do you think we got her to discover her core callings? What did we do right that she could finally confront her inner desires? Why do you think she felt connected with us?

I would like you to think of negotiation as a spotlight game. Imagine you and your counterpart are sitting on either side of the table and there is a spotlight on top. The spotlight always shines on the person who speaks. If you are speaking, then the spotlight in on you. If the counterpart is speaking, then the spotlight is on her. Who do you think should the spotlight be on? You or your counterpart? Obviously your counterpart. She needs to feel important. She needs to feel connected. She needs to feel in control of what she wants. But how do you get your counterpart to feel in control? How do you get her to give you something that you need?

The answer is focus questions. Questions that make the counterpart feel in control and yet help you achieve your goals. Questions that makes your counterpart feel like they are in the driver's seat and yet it is you who us feeding her the directions.

Before getting into focus questions, let us dwell a bit about questions in general. What is the need to ask questions? In a negotiation, acting dumb is a smart strategy. Playing stupid and winning smart is an effective advice for all negotiators. Rather than assuming, questions give your counterpart an opportunity to explain themselves and reveal information in the process. Never assume anything. Until it is explicitly stated by the counterpart.

Most of us do not know how to ask questions. We are taught from childhood to answer questions and that is why, we haven't sharpened our questioning skills. As discussed earlier, there are 2 systems in the human brain – system 1 which is instinctive and emotional; and system 2 which is logical and evidence-driven. Most decisions that we take are emotional. After we take an emotional decision, we use logic to justify ourselves. That is why we have to get the counterpart to grasp a clear idea of why he wants to do what he wants to do. Questions help us get the counterpart to open up and reveal their vision. Broadly, questions have two purposes: One, help the counterpart realize the realities and emotions that impact and influence the negotiation. And two, to drive the counterpart to an agreeable solution.

There are two categories of questions – the verb-led questions and the interrogative questions.

A verb-led question is one that starts with a verb – 'Can', 'Is', 'Do', 'Are' and so on. For example, look at the following questions:

"Can you do this?"

"Is this a good time to talk?"

"Do you want to place an order for this product?"

"Are you ready to sign the agreement?"

Most of such questions are closed questions, where the answer is 'yes', 'no' or worse 'maybe' as we discussed earlier. 'Maybe' gives you no clue where your counterpart stands. 'Yes' can be a fake yes and signal no actual commitment. If we are pushing the counterpart to a solution and forcing them to say 'yes', the negotiation backfires sooner or later. The only answer which is real is 'no' but that does not help your case. These are called closed-ended questions because there are only three predictable ways to answer the questions.

Also, look at questions like this: "Are you ready to do this?" versus "Aren't you ready to do this?"

Both forms are bad. Both are closed-ended questions. But the second one is particularly worse. The second one forces the counterpart to make a decision right now. It rushes the counterpart which in turn signals our neediness for the deal. Remember the chapter on need versus want? As we saw in the chapter on 'No', we always give the counterpart the open offer to say 'No'. We invite a 'No' at every step. We tell them it is okay to say 'No' anytime during the deal.

Another example of a bad question is "All of you know this, don't you?"

Here, the defenses shoot up crazily. I have heard countless trainers and coaches start with this. For example, "All of you are aware of the 80-20 principle, don't you?" When a coach asks this question to the audience, the only answer you get is a blank face if the counterpart doesn't know. The counterpart hides his ignorance in fear of embarrassment. This is a loaded question that can rub the listeners in a very wrong way.

At the opposite end of the spectrum are interrogative questions. These are questions that start with 'How', 'What', 'Why', "When', 'Who', 'Which' and 'Where'. These are open-ended questions where the answer cannot be given in 'yes', 'no', or 'maybe'. These require the counterpart to give away some information. These questions are a means of discovery, a means of unraveling more information and a means to get more details. These are called 'interrogative' questions because they interrogate.

For a negotiator, the preferred interrogative questions are the ones with 'How' and 'What' plus an occasional touch of 'Why'. The others are important but they do not lead to more elaborate answers. This is the trio that you have to master. Think of the question "What do you want me to do in this situation?" or "How will this deal affect the way we do business?" The answer to the question cannot be given without understanding the core issue. It needs a thorough explanation, and stating what the counterpart feels is a possible explanation to the question.

A step further is the focus questions, where we take interrogative questions and ask them in a way to get the counterpart closer to our objective. If we go to Rekha's journey at the beginning of this chapter, you will see a lot of focus questions that we asked her to get to the core.

"What if you can convert your hobby to a business?" – this question was to get Rekha to start looking inward and find the real motivation behind learning something. We could have taken things at face value when she said she wanted to spend some time learning a hobby, but always dig deeper. This is where we nudge the prospect and get her to see the value of starting her own business. She hadn't come to the discussion with a mindset of starting a business. But, we wanted to check out if she was willing to consider that option.

After rehashing and acknowledging some of her underlying feelings and once the empathetic connect was established, we ask "How can I help to make today better?" That is driving to the core. That is a strongly worded focus question that makes the counterpart think about their real wants and needs. What does she really want 'today'? This is where she tells us what is driving her to her decisions. Often, the counterpart will herself not have clarity of her core needs. Each focus question gets us there.

Suppose for a moment, we asked "Do you want to start the course now?" The answer would, in all probabilities be "Maybe, I don't know. Let me go back home and decide." Because, the prospect has not yet figured out her pain points.

A deeper connotation in asking focus questions is to gently guide your counterpart in the way that you want the negotiations to proceed and yet give her a feeling of controlling the direction and momentum of the conversation. It is 'your' solution that they are driving at. The best

Focus Questions

negotiation is one where your counterpart convinces herself that your ask is what she always wanted. When you ask focused questions, you tap into the natural inclination of people to help those they feel are less informed or less intelligent. It makes them feel important. It boosts their ego. It makes them feel in control of the situation. It makes the negotiation all about them. It is okay if you don't feel important in the negotiation as long as you get what you want. You are not in the negotiation to feel good. I cannot stress this point any further.

And again a disclaimer: Use the sincere deep tone that makes this look like a request.

Example of focused question:

- "How can both of us gain value through this deal?"
- "What did you mean when you said '…'"
- "How can we add value to the deal?"
- "What are our key constraints that need to be hashed out before proceeding?"
- "How can we solve the problem?"
- "What type of products are you looking for in this segment?"
- "I am not sure if I have been able to understand clearly. Would you mind explaining them once again?"
- "I know that the price that you have quoted is after deliberating on sound facts, but for some reason I am not getting it. Can you explain to me how you finalized these numbers?"
- "We have been having these arguments for a long time but we aren't going anywhere. What can we do to solve the issues together?"
- "How am I supposed to do that?"
- "What part of my proposal gives you the most concern?"

- "What can we do to get more business from you?"

Focus specifically on the 'how' based questions. If you use it subtly, a 'how' question will often seem like a request for clarification. For example, "how can we help here?" in a soft tone is different from "HOW CAN WE HELP HERE?" with a loud glaring tone. The latter is an expression of anger and frustration. The former is a request for help. If delivered in the right tone with the right words, they will feel like an appeal rather than an interrogation.

After 'what' and 'how' we are left with 'why' questions. Always remember to ask a 'why' question when the why is in your favor. Suppose you have pitched to a prospective company to become a vendor and they have asked you to come down for a discussion. You can ask "Why would you want to discuss this proposition with us when you already have an existing vendor?" This 'why' is directed in your favor. Or, if somebody is trying to pitch you against a competitor, you may ask "If you have already got a lower price offer, why are you not taking it from them?"

I was standing in line to get coffee at a local coffee shop. The person at the head of the line ordered some coffee and pulled out an INR 2000 note. The cashier at the counter looked perplexed – it was difficult to get change for such a high denomination note. He asked if the customer had change.

The customer shouted back "If I had change, why wouldn't I give it to you in the first place?" That is a loaded question. That is an insult. It is really not helpful when you are at the defending end. He snatched the INR 2000 off the cashier's hand and stormed out of the coffee shop, obviously without the coffee.

The customer next-in-line approached the cashier and said "I am so sorry, but I think I have the same problem as the last person. I checked my wallet but I can only see a INR 2000 denomination note. I understand that it might be difficult for you to find change but I am not sure what I can do. Can you help me?"

The cashier looked at him with compassion and said, "Let me see what I can do." He went inside with the INR 2000 note, spoke to some of his colleagues and got the change he needed. The customer walked away with the coffee and change. What he did was build empathy, acknowledge the subtle feeling that the cashier might have, use an apology to anchor his emotions and only then ask for help with a focus question. "Can you help me?" is a wonderful focus question that gets your counterpart to focus on you and think on your behalf. You do not need to show your importance in the negotiation. It is not a power game. It is driving the counterpart to believe that he has to help you.

HOW TO WIN BACK A CLIENT FROM THE COMPETITOR

Gaurav Agarwal ran a small trading business from his home in Siliguri. He supplied paper and stationery to educational organizations and businesses across the city. It was an aggressive market and there was always more supply than demand. The competition was cut-throat and traders were always finding new ways to cut out the competition. He started this business 12 years ago when he was 29 years and built his business from scratch. He knew in and out of the paper trading industry, market seasonality, fluctuations, supply chain bottlenecks and customer demands on the back of his palm. Though the market, in general, had been good that year, he found a significant dip in orders from one particular customer. He had noticed it last month as well, but ignored it as a one-off. Now there was a dip again this month. That was unusual. He fixed up a meeting with this customer.

Gaurav was a hardworking businessman. He was honest with his business and always strived to protect his reputation. "Reputation is the only competitive edge that you have in such a demanding market," he had once told me in a business meeting. He had excellent records of supplying to his customers on time. He even had the reputation of returning any excess amount if clients paid by mistake. This incident was narrated by Gaurav and shows the power of focus questions.

He walked into the client's office. After exchanging pleasantries, Gaurav said, "We are seeing some low order numbers from your business for the past two months. Is there some change that is happening in your business?"

"No," came the one-word reply. That was expected. Gaurav's had asked a verb-led question.

Gaurav probed further, "Last month, we received orders for 35 reams of paper instead of your usual 62 reams per month. This month, it is even lower at 28 reams. I am unable to comprehend the sudden dip in the orders. Could you please guide me on what challenges you are facing?" This time, he asked a focus question.

"There aren't any challenges, just that business is difficult these few months," said the customer looking away. One thing that negotiators learn from experience is that a person not able to maintain eye contact when answering a direct question needs to be probed further. In some cases, it might be a genuine habit of the person, but in most cases, it is an attempt to hide or misguide.

"Sir, we have been a long-standing supplier for you and have been with you for a long time. We understand that businesses go through challenging times and we are here to support you as much as possible. However, our analysis of the market shows that the sector you are in is doing good this year and our clients in similar businesses have increased their orders by up to 20%," Gaurav said subtly, calling out the lie.

"What can we do to get more business from you?" Again a focus question in a deep sincere tone. Followed by a long dynamic silence. This looks like a question but feels like a request. It is as if we are asking for help.

The customer was caught up in a bind. His facial muscles twitched.

Finally, he relented "See, you are charging a lot more than competitors. I have received a lower quotation and am moving some orders to them."

Gaurav mirrored, "a lot more than competitors?"

"Yes, I have got rates 5% lower than your pricing. With so many reams of paper getting ordered every month, it saves a lot of cost for us," replied the customer.

Gaurav knew that the competitor was giving a lower price just to onboard the customer. Margins are low in this business and this 5% discounted price cannot hold up for long. Sooner or later, they will increase the price.

"You are saying that you have received a quote from a competitor who is charging 5% less than us. It seems that you feel our prices are not competitive enough." Gaurav rehashed and acknowledged the customer's point.

"That is correct. If you can reduce the price we can work with you, else we have to shift the entire business to competition." An ultimatum by the customer.

Gaurav ignored the ultimatum and cut through to the core. "It seems you feel displeased regarding our pricing. Both of us have been working together for the past many years and we are eager to find a solution on this front. Our pricing is very competitive compared to the market and cover a lot of incidental costs like delivery and handling. Having said that, we would like to continue to work with you. What do you need to feel that we are committed to your business?" The third focus question.

"You have to give us something without which this relationship will not work out," said the customer.

Gaurav knew that the customer spent significant time and money on maintaining a proper storage space for the paper reams. He countered, "Sir, our offer is very competitive and you have seen that in so many years of working together, we have never failed a commitment or broken your trust. We have always worked with you to benefit your business. We would not commit a price that we cannot keep up. However, we will break down the delivery of reams into smaller quantities and deliver on a fortnightly basis rather than on monthly basis to help you save the maintenance costs."

Smart move. Gaurav's delivery team visited the location regularly to cater to other businesses. One additional delivery wouldn't be a challenge. A very nominal cost for him but substantial savings for the customer. Relationship saved.

Gaurav did not come up with a solution directly and offer the 5% discount. That would have started a price war – something that he wanted to avoid. He continued to connect with the customer through active listening, rehashing and acknowledging his feelings and working past the ultimatum. He asked several focus questions to guide the conversation gently to an area where something mutual can be worked out. And importantly, he made the customer feel important. It was as if the customer was controlling the conversation all through.

WHEN YOU FALL IN LOVE

Take a hypothetical example of a sales conversation. The salesperson pitches a product at INR 1000. You give a counteroffer of INR 800. He then gives reduces his price to INR 900. You counter with an increased amount of INR 850. And so on, it usually goes. What happens here is that for every discount the salesperson makes, he expects you to reciprocate and increase your counteroffer. If you don't reciprocate, you break the fundamental social norms of reciprocation. Or, if you directly tell them 'No', the salesperson may feel offended and walk away. You would, then, be left with one less option. And, the lower the number of options, the more stressful the negotiations become. So, how do you say 'No' to the initial offers and yet keep the counterpart giving you discounts? How do you get them to bid against themselves?

I remember this incident that happened some years back when I was shopping for a suit. This was not the standard retail clothing chain but a specialty store where they customized suits accordingly to the buyer's preferences. While browsing through some options, my eyes fell on this one particular suit tucked away behind a glass shelf and immediately fell in love with that. It was a gorgeous wrinkle-free honeycomb grey suit with black buttons. The moment I saw the suit I was taken. This suit had an oomph about it. I had to buy it.

When as a buyer, I have to have a product, my wants turn into needs. A needy person in front of a hungry salesperson is like meat in front of a tiger. You are just waiting to be pounced upon. I breathed in deeply and started my negotiation.

"How much is that for?"

The salesperson thought he had me and started explaining the product in detail, about the comfort levels of the material, wrinkle-free quality, colour combination and how rare it was to find a honeycomb suit in the market. He ended with "This would cost you INR 15000."

I wasn't aware of the exact margin of the product, but knew for sure that clothing retails had a wide margin, especially the specialty ones. And the honeycomb suit was a bit different from normal suits. There wouldn't be many takers for it. If the salesperson lost me on this deal, he may have to wait for a long time for another buyer. So, instead of giving a counteroffer, I let the salesperson give me another offer.

"Yes, this is a beautiful suit," I smiled back at the salesperson, "But I don't have such a budget, will you be having any discount on this?"

The salesperson continued with the normal pitch about the suit and added, "We can give you a 10% discount on this."

"I love the suit and I want to purchase it right away. I appreciate your discount, but that is still beyond by budget. I am sorry, but I won't be able to afford that amount for this suit."

"Do you have a budget in mind?" he asked.

I countered with a low-ball offer of INR 8000 to anchor him and get his to come down to his minimum. "I can pay in cash and in full immediately," I added.

The salesperson got the shock of a lifetime. He blinked his eyes and stopped to recollect his thought. "I don't think that would be possible. You can finance the purchase by credit card - we have a EMI options for cards which would be charged monthly for you."

"This suit looks stunning; I really want to take his today. Maybe it is worth much more than what I can offer. I am sorry but I cannot afford to pay more." I brought in more empathy and resonated with him.

The anchor worked. After some pause, he said, "Sir, I can give this to you at INR 11000 full and final."

"It is a bit of an embarrassment for me to ask you for discounts, but this number doesn't work for me. I wish I had more budget for this. I really can't pull in any more. How can I pay that much?" I ended with a focus question. The trick to a focus question is to make it look like a request than an ask.

Now was the time to put in the dynamic silence. I let him feel that void. He fidgeted. The silence was uncomfortable. Finally, he said, "Let me check with the store manager."

After about ten minutes, he came back. "INR 10,000," he said without looking me in the eye.

"You have really helped me a lot. You have been kind enough to hear me. But all I have is INR 8000 in cash right now," I said pulling out the notes, "and about INR 962 in my digital wallet. That's all I can give."

Moments later, I walked out with this gorgeous honeycomb suit brought at INR 8962. The suit is still there with me.

SAYING NO WITHOUT HURTING

Here is a 6-step process to saying NO without hurting:

1. Apologize – to take away the inherent accusations that may come
2. Resonate – Rehash and Acknowledge – to build more empathy
3. Dynamic Silence – to build the pressure
4. Focus Questions – to get them to bid against themselves
5. Smile – And they are forced to reciprocate
6. Repeat

WHAT NOT TO DO DURING FOCUS QUESTIONS

Don't show off your vocabulary: Make your questions as short and to the point as possible. Make it clear and crisp. Make it as easily digestible as possible. Don't make a question like a thesis – with long, arduous and complex words. You don't want to show your vocabulary. Your objective is to get more information. Something that the counterpart can process easily and answer effectively.

Don't vomit questions: Ask questions one by one. Since negotiations are inherently stressful, a lot of times we start vomiting questions one after the other. We have so much to ask that we load one question on another without a pause. Instead, take one question at a time and wait for the counterpart to explain it. Follow questions with mirrors or flips to get them to reveal in-depth. Then ask the next question. Your objective is to know as much as possible.

Don't talk too much: Another mistake we do in questioning is not pausing long enough after the question. A pause or a dynamic silence allows the counterpart to think about what we just asked. Any talking during this phase will dilute the counterpart's thought process and maybe influence it. Use silence to your advantage. Let your counterpart fill in the silence with his answers. Rookie negotiators do something like this: "Why do you want to do that?" you ask. And then follow it up with "While you are trying to figure that out, let me outline the next point in the agenda…" You have taken away the need for your counterpart to answer the question.

Don't answer the question for them: The final mistake follows from the earlier point. We start with a good question for the counterpart and then answer the question on their behalf. For example, "What part of my proposal gives you the most concern?" and then follow it up with "Is it the pricing or the delivery terms?" What you have fundamentally done is answer your own question and made it easier for the counterpart to dodge or answer with as nominal information as possible. Avoid the temptation to elaborate.

CHAPTER SUMMARY

In any negotiation, playing dump is a smart strategy. The person who listens always has a bigger advantage over the person who talks. The person talking is divulging information. We have seen in the past few chapters how we can use active listening to unearth a lot more information about the counterpart. How else can you get the counterpart to reveal more? Here are some key takeaways from this chapter:

- Use focus questions to get your counterpart to open up more. Focus question gets your counterpart to focus on sharing information that you want and would be beneficial to the negotiation. Interrogative questions starting with What, How and Why will give you perspective on the counterpart's stance.

- Focus questions makes your counterpart feel in control. It gives them the false sense of being in the driver's seat when it is you who is giving the instructions on which direction to go.

Focus Questions

- Use What and How to get details about the counterpart's position. These are to be mostly used.

- Use why when the why favors you and you want the counterpart to tell you the reason they are still talking to you or dealing with you.

- Avoid verb-led questions unless absolutely necessary. Never use verb-led questions that can be answered in a one-word answer like 'Yes' or 'No'.

- Avoid questions that force your counterpart into agreeing with you like "Shouldn't you do this?" or "Don't you agree to this?"

- Use a softening phrase like "It seems" or "Perhaps" or "Maybe". Make the question look like a request rather than an interrogation. You will get much better responses with clarity from the counterpart regarding their position.

TIME TALES

My father loves bargaining. He bargains hard. He has this instinctive tendency to get the best price for purchases. Everywhere he goes, every shop he visits, he pushes for the lowest possible price. If it is a commodity, he visits multiple sellers for the same product, gauges the ideal lowest price for that item and then buys it.

It was a chilly December winter morning. About 9 AM. My parents had just landed at the airport and I was there to pick them up. They had gone for a family trip to South India for a fortnight. It was a packed trip – they visited five cities in three states, mostly took the train, bus or cabs for hopping between cities, often not staying at a particular location for more than couple of days. The return flight was from Chennai.

I could feel their exhaustion the moment they came out from the arrival gates. After collecting the luggage, we walked to the taxi aisle. This was during the early phase of ride-share apps. Not many people were accustomed to ordering cabs through apps. It was still the hay days of the yellow taxis in Kolkata.

Time Tales

I hailed a taxi and popped my head in through the passenger side window. "How much to go to Salt Lake?"

"INR 500," the driver said nonchalantly.

My father shoved me aside, "Why are you charging INR 500? The normal price is just INR 200."

"INR 400," pat came the response.

"That is still high. The last price we will give is INR 250." My father retorted.

"INR 300. Final charge," the driver was indifferent.

"No, INR 250 is what we will give you," my father said.

The driver started the taxi and drove off.

My father hailed another taxi and told him the destination. The driver started at INR 400 – a better initial offer than the earlier driver. My father responded with INR 200, the driver countered with INR 300. As I said earlier, my father loves a hard bargain. He responded with INR 250. The driver ignored him and drive off.

You can't be more tenacious than my father. He hailed the next taxi and started all over again. My mother was standing next to him and listening attentively as the bargains were playing out. Before he started negotiating, she said, "I am tired after so much of travel. I will give you INR 50 if that will seal the deal. Let's go home as quickly as possible." My father started explaining the optimal pricing and how taxis are fleecing customers. But soon realized that while he was trying to save INR 50, he was ignoring the value of time.

As negotiators, we are so focused on getting the perfect deal and winning that we ignore the value of time and energy that goes into pursuing the victory. In doing so, negotiators often waste a lot of vital time on non-critical and trivial negotiations. That time could have been utilized for other deals, or better tasks or unwinding. Many negotiators are so focused like horses-on-blinders that they miss out on the bigger picture. Is that extra INR 50 worth it? Is that extra 1-day early delivery important to spend time negotiating?

For a rookie negotiator, time is essentially a free commodity that can be given out generously, so he spends time doing things that do not add value or even worse takes away value from what he does. If you feel you have all the time in this world, think of better things that can be done – where your efforts will lead to higher payoffs. Focus more on improving your critical negotiations and less on trivial items. It is a mindset change – one that will take time to implement. We have been conditioned to make such mistakes that it will take conscious effort to get over this habit.

Take this simple example. If a colleague comes up to you and says, "Do you have a minute?", our automatic response is "Yes, tell me". We proceed to keep aside whatever work we were doing to listen to her. Or, if someone in your department has set up a meeting for 30 minutes, the first response would be to accept the invite. These are small instances that left unchecked can blow out of proportions. The mind is like a muscle, the more you exercise it, the stronger it becomes. You would want to start with such simple cases to build your willpower to resist other eating up your schedule.

AMPLIFYING YOUR COUNTERPART'S TIME COSTS

Let us come back to negotiations and look at it from a different perspective – the cost of time spent by the counterpart. A good negotiator will use time as a tool to win negotiations. Instead of eating away his own time, he will use the counterpart's time to his advantage. He will start working on amplifying the counterpart's time cost to put artificial pressure. Tactics like asking someone to send a detailed mail with brochure are amplifying their time costs and getting the person invested in the process more deeply. Or, asking the counterpart to drive a long distance or fly down for a meeting. Or, putting him on hold for five minutes before connecting.

We learned it the hard way. There was this prospect we were trying to onboard as a client. Getting through to him was a challenge. His secretary would receive the call, put us on hold for two minutes before saying that he wasn't available, but always politely asked us to call back a day later. We had earlier got an initial meeting with him and based on the discussion, we had sent him a proposal and quotation over email. This deal was important. We were adamant to get through to him. Violation number one – we became needy.

After more such failed calls, we decided to visit him directly. When we reached, we were told that he was in a meeting, but his secretary said he would be free for ten minutes the next day post-lunch and that she could sneak us in. "Don't tell my boss that I have told you about the free time," she winked at us. Huh! We got ourselves an advantage and we will finally catch him off-guard. We were excited. Violation number two – we developed positive expectation.

The next day, we prepared our speech and reached his office. Sure enough, his secretary let us in post-lunch. "Hi, what a surprise to see you guys here?" the prospect exclaimed, "What brings you here?"

"Sir, we had sent the email to you. Did you have a chance to look at it?"

"Err…Yes, I think I saw it but then something important came up and hand to rush. Let me pull it out," he towered over his laptop. "Here it is. Let me go through it." He seemed to scan the document and then said, "This is way too high a quotation. I have got a couple of more proposals at half this value. Discuss this with your office and call my secretary when you are ready."

A sense of desperation came over me. Again following up with the secretary multiple times, not getting appointments, traveling to his office was a wastage of time and energy. I had an internal price cutoff at 55% of the quoted price. So, we decided to quote at 60% and get this over with. Violation number three - getting hijacked by an extreme anchor.

"Sir, I can only go down to 60% of the quoted price. That is our internal cutoff."

"Hmm," he thought for a few seconds, "okay, we will do it. Meet my secretary – she will do the formalities." I walked out of the room not-quite-happy but pleased to have got myself a deal.

Weeks later, we found out that this was his negotiating style. He, along with his secretary, played this game of amplifying his counterpart's time costs to such an extent that they will be willing to sign the deal at desperately low prices just to break out from the vicious cycle of discomfort. Would we have agreed normally to sign at such ridiculously low prices? Hell, no! But when we are drained of energy and lost significant time, we become desperate. We try to save ourselves the misery.

This is not an isolated incident. Such occurrences happen all the time.

Another way of counterparts amplifying your time costs is when they say "I have just ten minutes before I jump into another meeting. Show me what you have to show." And in the heat of the moment, you blurt out all information, pricing, terms and everything else associated with the deal. You don't ask focused questions, you don't listen, you don't discover their why. You feel that you have to convince the counterpart with whatever you have and get him to close the deal in ten minutes. That never happens. Your counterpart gets away with all the data leaving you at a disadvantage. The only way to deal with such a scenario is to say, "Sir, thank you for taking out time today. What I was about to show you would take more than ten minutes. I can come back another day when you are free and we will demonstrate our offering. When would be a good time to call you for fixing the appointment." So, no neediness on your part. You put the onus on your counterpart.

Every minute spent by you negotiating at the table is a minute spent also by your counterpart. Simple but revolutionary concept. Use that concept to amplify your counterpart's time cost. You can do it by canceled meetings and delayed response to emails or missed phone calls. The most effective way to negotiate is not to start the negotiation unless and until you know that the prospect is ready to make the decision and that it needs to be done in a short amount of time.

DEADLINES

An interesting notion that emanates from time is the idea of a deadline. A deadline is an artificial time limit by which the deal has to be made. It is imaginary and almost always deadlines can be moved, changed or eliminated. The idea of a deadline is to put pressure on either side to close the deal. When you think of a deadline what feelings come to your mind? It is anxiety and pressure. Why? Because of the perceived loss that if the deadline crosses then the deal will fall through. So, we rush to close a deal even if the outcome is worse than no deal at all. The notion is to use deadlines to our advantage; and resist our urge to give into deadlines imposed by others.

During coaching we play negotiation simulations as a way to get the participants to imbibe certain concepts. We set up the simulation and give them ten minutes to find a solution through negotiation, repeating all the while that a conclusion must be reached within the deadline. While the participants are busy with the negotiation, we stroll around the hall eavesdropping on what and how they are doing. For the first eight minutes, we see participants trying to block each other, asking questions, arguing on details and trying to counter the others. No decision had been reached. And then we announce that only two minutes are left. That triggers a flurry of concessions in those last few minutes and the deal gets hammered out.

Herb Cohen, an expert American negotiator shared a story of the perils of deadline. His company had sent him to Japan to negotiate his first big business deal. When he landed in Japan, his counterparts asked him how long he would be in Japan. Cohen told them he will be there for a week. For the next seven days, his hosts entertained him with parties, tours and outings. His Japanese counterparts did not even broach the subject of the deal during those seven days. On the final day, when Cohen was leaving for the airport, they started discussing the deal and finalized the terms in the car on the way to the airport. Cohen was sure that the agreed deal favored the other side and that he has been played. He had conceded too much just to make the deal before the deadline.

In negotiations, a thumb rule is that 80 percent of the concessions are done in the last 20 percent of the time. That is when the pressure mounts to close the deal. When demands are brought to the table early on, neither party would be willing to concede. But when demands are presented late, both sides are willing to make significant concessions to make the deal. As time winds down, both sides are forced to make a decision.

Everything in negotiation is negotiable, which means deadlines are also negotiable. We have never come across a situation where deadlines have caused a deal to fall through which otherwise would have been a great deal. If a deal is productive for both parties, then a deadline can be negotiated.

A very good example where both sides know about the deadline is renewing rental or lease agreements. Let us say your rental is up for renewal in five months and you must negotiate with your landlord. You may think "I will use the pressure of a deadline to get the best deal. If I don't continue here and vacate this office, the landlord may have to keep the premises vacant for a few months before he can find a tenant. That will put him under time pressure." This is great until you realize that a similar strategy can be used by your landlord on you.

So, there is a known time frame and both sides are approaching the same deadline. Which side should put the time pressure tactics? Well the answer is whichever side has the most power. The party with the most power will use the deadline tactic and the other party with lesser power either has to concede or try to get onto the negotiating table as early as possible. The next question is which side has the most power? The answer is the party with the most alternate options hold greater power. What do you do? You start listing all the alternate options that you or the landlord have if the deal falls through.

For you, it will be: What are the alternate locations? What are their rental costs? If you are a retail outlet, are your customers in that area? Will it be easy and cost-effective to move to that location? What are the other operational issues of working from the alternate location? How long do you or others have to travel to reach the office daily? And so on.

For the landlord it will be: How long will he wait before he gets a tenant? Will the rental be lesser or more than the current amount? What is the cost of repainting? Will this location be easily marketable?

Since you are fully aware of your costs and constraints without full knowledge of the landlord's, you either start having positive expectations or negative expectations depending on your research. Best is to take an objective view, though easier said than done. If still, you find out that your position is weaker than the best option is to start early negotiation. But, if your landlord's position is weaker, you can delay the negotiation till the very end.

SHOULD YOU REVEAL YOUR DEADLINE?

Deadline is a two-way street. There are often cases where the negotiation takes place for days and months without coming close to a solution. Some tough opponents would use the delay tactics to amplify your time costs and get you to cave into their demands out of sheer frustration. The best way to speed up a negotiation is to let the other party know about your deadline. While a deadline reduces your freedom to maneuver, it puts the counterpart under immense pressure to close the deal. If they feel that you will walk away if things don't close within the deadline, then they will start coming to the real issues. If you walk away from a deal, the counterpart also does not get the deal. It is their loss as well since they have also invested time and energy into the discussions. When the negotiation is over for one side, it is over for the other side as well.

When you reveal your final deadline, you get better deals. Why? Because it does two things:

1. Both sides work hard to getting a deal before the deadline. It reduces your chance of walking away without a deal.
2. When the opponent knows your deadline, he will start making concessions early.

In Cohen's story earlier, if he would have left without making a deal, that would have also been a loss for the Japanese company. Or if he would have extended his stay, he could have made a better deal. When negotiation is terminated by one side, it is over for the other side as well. Cohen's neediness to make the deal at any cost led to an extremely unfavorable deal.

Finally, do not confuse time costs with deadlines. Though they look similar, they are different in the way they impact the parties involved. Deadlines affect both sides in the negotiation. If deadlines are over, then both party gets affected. However, time costs apply to one party only. For instance, your counterpart is stalling the negotiation and waiting for the last moment to get more deals (like we saw earlier in the chapter with the prospect and the secretary). These are time costs on your side which the counterpart is trying to exploit. To get leverage on the situation and get the counterpart to take notice, impose a final deadline by when the things should be hammered out. If the counterpart feels that if the deal is not sealed by a deadline, then it will fall through and the deal is good enough to warrant more discussion, he will come back with some concessions or agree to a discussion.

One question that always comes up is what someone has to do when they are up against a deadline which is particularly not in their favor. More than what is to be done is what isn't to be done. Deadlines are psychological pressures – so the first thing is not to give off any physical signs that you are tensed – like shaking legs, pacing the room, fretting or getting angry on others. These are tell-tale signs that you have been cornered. You do not want to give the feeling to the counterpart that you are under pressure. If they get that feeling, then they will start asking for more concessions from you and which will affect your deal even worse. Best is to remain calm and composed and show the counterpart that you are not daunted by the upcoming deadline.

USING TIME TO YOUR ADVANTAGE

Getting the best deal may not always be about features or price. It is about letting the other person feel the loss if the deal does not go through. What better way to do that than using time to our advantage! When you use time to trigger feelings of anxiety and loss, your counterpart kicks aside logic and tries to rush to close the deal. The same may happen to you as well. So, resist the urge to give in to deadlines. While below points seems to be manipulative, these are used by many negotiators to get a deal:

1. Let deadlines breathe down their neck: The best situation to be in is when you don't have an urgency to close the deal but your counterpart has a strict deadline. Think of a salesperson trying to close a deal just before the month-end. If it isn't urgent, you can hold back for a few more days. But for the salesperson, if

the deal doesn't go through, he will lose out on target and in essence his bonus. So, more often than not, he will concede to discounts, terms favorable for you, additional features, special gifts and more.

2. Make time your ally: Get your counterpart to invest time and energy in making the deal work. Like traveling multiple times to your office, writing out long contracts, getting the counterpart to hold onto the line before getting connected or rewriting changes part by part over time.

3. Get into a meeting with a short time frame: Let the counterpart know that you are in the meeting for a very short period and that you have another meeting immediately post this. This will make inexperienced negotiators spill out crucial information. If the meeting needs to be extended, you can always reschedule the imaginary second meeting.

4. Withhold critical decision-makers from the early stage negotiation: Once the counterpart has taken you through the deal details, reveal that there are other decision makers who need to be informed. Get the counterpart to come down again to meet the other decision-makers.

5. Inform the counterpart of your deadlines: Be ready to walk away if deals don't close during the prescribed time frame. You would rather spend the time on other critical activities which may have a bigger payout than the ongoing negotiation.

VETTING THE PROCESS

Vikas Kumar was the co-founder of an emerging startup and also a participant from one of our negotiation coaching batches. His startup had been on a growing spree for the past 12 months and was looking to raise INR 5 crores to fuel their growth for the next 18 months. After meeting with many investors, they finally found one who was willing to invest in their startup. Vikas's burn rate was not very high, but they had to complete raising the next round within 3-4 months.

After the initial few rounds of discussion, both sides decided to go ahead with the deal. Vikas along with his CFO prepared the documents and on the said day came to meet the investor for signing the contract. When they entered the board room, he was shocked to see the investor flanked with bankers and lawyers. After they were seated, the bankers started renegotiating the amount. They proposed two options - a lower amount for the same equity or alternatively, more equity at the same investment. Vikas was not comfortable with either. If he agreed, his valuation would be a lot less than what he projected. They had worked hard to get to this point and did not want to lose valuation now.

The lawyers started modifying the terms of the deal, exclusivity clause, preferred share terms and right of first refusal. Vikas was now flabbergasted. He did not expect the last moment attacks. He did not want to give in to the last-minute demands. He attempted to convey that the deal details had already been finalized but to no avail.

Had he just wasted weeks of negotiation in vain? Had he made a mistake during the initial discussions to understand the intent of the investor? Was there something in the documents that he hadn't read carefully? Or was he being pressured by the lawyers and bankers to sweeten the deal? Did the investor just want to check out the startup without any intention to invest?

Utterly frustrated with what was happening, Vikas said, "I am so sorry but we are unable to understand the last-minute changes that are happening. It may have been a mistake on our part and our understanding of the discussions. We were under the impression that the deal details were discussed and we had agreed to go ahead with the investment. The proposals laid out today deviate significantly from our early talks and would severely affect our valuations. However, we are sorry that the new terms would not do justice to our effort. We had prepared the whole proposal and we would be extremely glad to continue with the deal on the initial terms."

After repeating his desire to do the deal on the initial terms, Vikas and his CFO excused themselves from the board room and left. This debacle would not have happened if Vikas and his team would have first discussed with the investor how to navigate the process of the negotiation. Even before starting to discuss the deal, Vikas should have ensured that both sides are clear as to how the negotiations would take place - who all will get involved at what stage, what are the key decision-making factors, a tentative timeline for the deal to close and so on.

This is called vetting the process even before the actual deal is discussed. And this is crucial to ensure that the negotiations flow smoothly irrespective of whether the deal is reached or not. Some of the preliminary things to discussion while vetting the process:

- Tentative timeline to close the deal.
- Who all will be involved in different stages of the negotiation process?
- Who all would be involved in finalizing the deal?
- Key factors that will influence the deal
- Intermediate milestones during the negotiation phase
- Agenda for each meet.
- How the deal discussion will flow?
- Who will have the power to decide on key elements?

The vetting process is crucial to save time and energy in making the deal. The more clarity there is in the process, the easier it becomes to negotiate critical terms in the deal. If Vikas was aware that the bankers would have a say in the valuation, he would have asked the investor to bring along the bankers in the early stage of the discussion. Though

Vikas did have a good ending. His gamble in leaving the boardroom paid off. The investor did not want to sour the milk. He called five days later and close the deal on initial terms.

NEGOTIATING WITH GATEKEEPERS

Anurag Mishra led the Institutional sales team at Simplex Textiles. Simplex, based out of Bhopal, manufactured fabrics and yarn and supplied to garment manufacturers. He had been in sales across companies for the past 15 years with a varied range of roles and experience. When he joined Simplex two years back, he was given only one goal – to ensure that the heads and decision-makers in major Garment Manufacturing Companies from Bhopal knew Simplex by name and was eager to place an order.

Simplex Textiles had been pitching to Muktar Garments, a clothing production house who manufactured garments and supplied to some of the popular big-box retailers. Every time they called Muktar Garments and asked to be connected to the Director; the assistant manager would intercept the call and create some hindrance. The assistant manager, Subhas Tekriwal would be asking for brochures, company profiles, a list of previous clients, technical expertise in ensuring product quality and so on. It was getting challenging for Anurag to control his urge to launch a verbal attack on Subhas. In every call, Subhas would come up with new questions and demands. This was going nowhere.

Subhas was a gatekeeper, or screener or blocker as they are called from time to time. They are people who guard the decision-makers and try to put in as much blockage as possible between you and the key person. Like we saw the secretary early in this chapter. They do not have much say in the negotiation but are there for impression management or to vet you or to insulate the key decision-makers.

At his wit's end, Subhas decided to try a different approach. Instead of thinking of Subhas as just another step before meeting the Director, he decided to involve him in the decision making process.

1. Humanize yourself:

A gatekeeper would probably get a lot of calls or emails asking for meetings or share proposals and marketing information. You wouldn't want to get lost in the crowd. Humanize yourself. Give a name to your voice. You don't want to sound like you do calling for a living. Don't ask for their names. Nobody likes to randomly handout their names to whoever calls on the line. Let them feel that you are a human being after all, someone who is non-threatening.

Anurag started the call, "Hello, this is Anurag from Simplex Textiles."

Not Anurag Mishra but Anurag. Do you call your friends by full name or only the first name? The first name, right. Similarly, using the first name makes you more humane and approachable. This is contrary to most business calls where you tell your full name and designation. But people are tired of random business calls. Next time, you are doing a tele call, start with your first name and see the difference.

2. Resonate and diffuse the negative:

The key to recruiting the gatekeeper is to play to his emotional needs. It is always a good approach to resonate with them, rehashing what they just said and acknowledging any feelings that might have seeped into the discussion. Let them feel important. Let them know that you value their inputs and opinion in the process.

Anurag continued, "I am so sorry to keep bothering you with calls. I know you are busy and have a lot on your hands and we don't want you to feel disturbed. Is this a bad time to talk?"

Look at the way he framed the statement. He packed in a lot of empathy and resonated with Subhas. He even used an apology to diffuse the negative even before Subhas could tell him that. When you remove the blame dynamics, you essentially remove the sting from their accusations. Finally, Anurag ended with a strongly worded No-oriented question to slightly nudge Subhas and give him a gentle ego massage.

3. Ask Focus Questions:

Demanding a meeting with decision-makers would not have a chance in such interactions. So, how do you get someone to help you? Ask focus questions. Let the gatekeeper feel in control of the discussion. Let him guide you to what you want.

Anurag continued, "I was wondering if you could let me know what we can do to meet with the Director."

He shot a focus question with a softening phrase. If you look at the structure, it seems like a request for help and not a direct question. This sentence treats Subhas with respect and deference and conveys that Anurag holds him in high esteem. It also signals to the power and influence that he has in the system. Treating a gatekeeper with disrespect can be catastrophic. He can simply block you or poison your image with the decision-maker.

4. Never take a No from someone who cannot give a Yes:

A gatekeeper's job is to say No. But they can never give you a yes, that is, yes to your proposal or the deal. But their opinions matter. A gatekeeper can block you by doing nothing or help your case by putting in a good word with the decision-maker. In many corporate business deals, the first person that you meet will never be the person making the decision. So, if a gatekeeper gives you a No, you can signal to him that you are not accepting the No, but do so in a very polite and agreeable way. Here are some examples of how Anurag can respond to a 'No' depending on the context:

- No-oriented question: "Would it be a bad idea to send an email to Director Sir and keep you in CC?"
- Resonate: "It seems that you have some reluctance in

communicating our proposal to the Director."

- Direct Mirror: "No? You don't want me to meet the Director?"

- Focus Question: "What can we do to get a meeting with the Director?" or "How can we present our proposal to the Director?" or "How do you suggest we meet the Director?"

These questions or statements indirectly tell the gatekeeper that you are not agreeing to what he is saying, yet keeping it so subtle and respectful. The voice tone also plays a role. Keep the soothing voice always with the gatekeepers.

5. End with gratitude:

Don't just bang down the phone if over call; or turn around and walk away if it is in-person. Make sure to end the conversation with the gatekeeper in a happy tone. You want that lingering after-taste of friendliness to get him to like you.

After the discussion, Anurag ended, "Thank you for helping me out. I am sorry if I took up much of your time. Would you mind if I give you a call next Tuesday when the Director is back in the office?"

6. Never burn your bridges:

Not only with gatekeepers but people in general. You never know who knows who. Or who becomes who. Keep the friendly feeling going with the gatekeeper. If you cause them to feel insulted, they would double down on you or foul mouth at any opportunity. Anurag did not get what he wanted in this call, but he started the process of making a connection with Subhas. This can and will give Simplex an advantage over its competitors. People are six times more likely to help you if they feel like they like you. The tone, delivery and approach can separate you from others. As the saying goes, make them like you and they will give their lives for you.

One final point. How do you know if someone is a gatekeeper or decision-maker? In a corporate setting, there are mazes of hierarchy and designations, how do you find out who makes the real decisions? The answer is that you cannot. So rather than assume, ask them. Use the vetting process described earlier to figure out who makes the real decisions. One thumb rule – If someone says "I" and "me" too many times, that person is likely to be a gatekeeper or someone who doesn't yield power. If the person says "they" or "us", you might be speaking to the decision-maker. Why? Because decision-makers want to create a distance between themselves and the decisions they make so that they can backtrack if ever necessary.

CHAPTER SUMMARY

In a negotiation, more often than not, we look at monetary terms, clauses, give and take philosophies and such intangibles, but we rarely take into account the time and energy that we spend in negotiating itself. Negotiation takes up a lot of time and we often have to figure out if the time getting invested in getting the best deal is worth the energy and time we put into it. Here are some key takeaways from this chapter:

- Amplify the time costs for your counterpart. Get them invested in the deal so that they cannot back away at the end citing frivolous reasons. If you are investing time in the deal, you must ensure that your counterpart is equally invested, else they can walk away with minimal impact leaving you stranded.

- Use deadlines to speed up the negotiation process. Deadline is a two-way street. If the negotiation ends for you, it ends for your counterpart as well. Let them know you have a deadline post which you have to look at alternatives.

- Most concessions are made in the last 20% of the time left before a deadline. Make this fact work for you.

- Ensure that you know who the real decision-makers are. Don't negotiate with someone who cannot give you a 'Yes' to the deal. Blockers and gatekeepers can often consume a lot of your time and energy without giving you real returns.

- Vet the process of negotiation before getting into the actual negotiation. Who will be there at the table? Who are the real decision-makers? Tentative timeline for the deal to close?

INFLUENCING STRATEGIES

Today was like no other day. Prakash Mathur was going for the deal of his life – a deal that could make him the top contender for the post of All India Sales Head for Prativa Engineers.

February 7, 2018, Wednesday. 9 AM. It was a bright sunny morning. There were heavy rains last night but the clouds had moved on leaving behind a sparkling white day. As a Regional Manager for Prativa Engineers, Prakash was in charge of the Western Region Sales with fifteen employees reporting to him. If this deal was successful, no one could stop him from getting promoted as the All India Sales Head. A position which till recently was held by Sameer Mukherjee, who got elevated a month back as the Vice President of the Company. The company was evaluating internal candidates for All India Sales Head position and Prakash was in the run along with two more candidates.

Prakash had started his career in sales when he was 21 years of age selling encyclopedias door-to-door. He did a lot of odd door-to-door sales jobs like water purifier sales, beauty and grooming products, insurance sales and a few more. He got the big break when he was spotted by Vimal Bansal, the promoter of Prativa Engineers when one day Prakash chanced upon his house selling water purifiers. Vimal was so impressed by his tenacity that he offered him a permanent job at his sales office in Birbhum, West Bengal. The pay was small, but it was a permanent job. Prakash gladly accepted.

From that small office, Prakash ground himself and paved his way to becoming what he was today. And if things went well today, he would become the preferred candidate for the All India Sales Head position. Today, he was meeting Dhananjay Bose, the Purchasing Director of Postcop Industries, one of the leading names in Food Packaging and Distribution in the country.

Prativa Engineers was a renowned manufacturer and supplier of a variety of precision-engineered Packaging Machines. Their products were premium quality and used the latest technology to design and manufacture export quality high-grade machines. Prakash had come to know that Postcop was looking for manufacturers of Aluminum Container Manufacturing Machine. Being one of the hallmark products of Prativa Engineers, it was a good fit for Postcop. Prakash had initiated the first meeting three months back pitching this product. Following the initial dialogue and specification gathering, Postcop had been delaying the decision-making process citing year-end closing and market scenarios. However, after tenacious follow-up, Postcop was finally ready to take the discussion to the next stage.

First things first. Prakash did not want to give Postcop any chance to stall the decision making any further. This has been dragging for some time and Prakash had to push them to make a decision. The only agenda he had for today's meeting was to discover the issues which were holding back Postcop and influence them to close the deal as quickly as possible. As we will see in this chapter, Prakash employs nine key influencing strategies which you too can use to leverage your position with the client. These strategies are to be used over and above the other negotiation techniques mentioned in the earlier chapters.

Sravan, junior manager at Postcop greeted Prakash at the reception and took him directly to Dhananjay's office.

"Hello Sir. Good Morning. How are you?' said Prakash handing over a small gift box to Dhananjay, "our Managing Director sends them for you. He had recently gone to Singapore for a meeting and had got a small gift for you. I think you will like it."

STRATEGY 1: PRESENT SYMBOLIC UNILATERAL CONCESSION

Some years ago in the USA, a trade association for construction subcontractors wanted to survey their members. Most members did not want to respond to survey questions. They were reluctant and did not have the incentive to fill out any questionnaires. In a bid to learn how to increase the response, the association decided to find out the power of financial incentives for filling out the survey. They divided the members into three groups. The first group was sent the questions with no financial incentive. Only 20% returned the completed questionnaire. The next group was promised a $50.00 payment for completing the survey. Unfortunately, the $50.00 incentive did not change the results significantly. Only 23% responded. One reason could be that $50.00 was not large enough an incentive. Maybe $100 or $200 would have let to better response rates. The third group was sent the survey form and along with it a $1.00 bill. This time 40% of members returned the completed survey.

This was shocking. Economic theories fail to explain why a $1.00 incentive worked - one, it way smaller than $50.00 incentive, and secondly, $1.00 was not really an incentive at all. What they found out was that $1.00 was not looked at as an incentive but rather a gift - which made the recipients feel obligated to reciprocate and respond.

What mattered was not the cost of the gift but the act of concession itself could induce reciprocity, compliance and agreement. Negotiators can use this strategy to start building up the pressure of reciprocity. The gifts or the concessions should be of absolutely nominal value. Some examples of token gifts and concessions that negotiators can use:

- Small gift of nominal cost but which would have been otherwise difficult to procure normally.
- Meeting the counterpart at his office or a time of his convenience.
- Giving up on very minor things without asking for anything in return.

Dhananjay smiled back, "Welcome to Postcop. And send my regards to Mr. Bansal." By giving the gift box to Dhananjay, he had started the cycle of reciprocation. Now Dhananjay has been put under pressure to reciprocate.

Dhananjay continued, "We understand that you wanted to discuss about taking the proposal forward. However, we have this year-end coming up and we may not be able to close the deal before that. Our expenses are frozen and there is hardly room for flexibility."

Anything that is not a direct 'No' means there is a shimmer of opportunity. Prakash sensed there could be ways he could fit in the purchase in Postcop's books before the year-end close.

Prakash rehashed, "As I understand, your year-end closing is coming up and you may not have enough time and budgetary flexibility to push the deal with management. Would it be okay if we can keep the discussion alive and go through the other points in the draft proposal that was prepared?"

"Okay. Let us visit the draft proposal and terms," Dhananjay agreed. Over the next few minutes they discussed the proposal and changes that can be done or improved in the technical specification.

When they were done with a part of the agenda, Prakash chipped in, "Sir, I was going through the latest market studies for your sector. It has been growing tremendously for the past few years and there has been a constant increase in demand. There is always more demand than you could cater to. The industry is at its peak and the market can absorb a lot more supply. If left unattended, a competitor might enter the market. Without this equipment, you stand to lose about INR 5 Crores of market revenue on an annual basis."

STRATEGY 2: EMPHASIZE POTENTIAL LOSSES RATHER THAN POTENTIAL GAINS

I was once taking a session at a company for about one hundred and ten participants on the topic of sales. It was the company's annual retreat and along with fun and games, the company wanted to refresh and polish sales skills for the front line people. The session was happening in a luxury hotel just outside Kolkata. It was chilling cold inside the hall. The hotel staff could not turn down the cooling due to equipment malfunction. So, every now and then, some participants were leaving the hall to relieve themselves, even though we already had scheduled bio-breaks. It was a chaotic situation and quite disturbing to see people walking across the hallway continuously. So, just before the next session started, I announced, "We are now going to show you something that can change your life. If you miss it, you will regret it for the rest of your life. If you miss it, you will lose out on Lakhs of revenue and with that your commission in the coming year." Not a single person left the hall during the next session.

People are more motivated to avoid losses than obtaining equivalent gains. This is called the principle of loss aversion. Even if the magnitude of losses or gains are the same, people are more inclined to act to prevent potential losses than to accumulate potential gains. Thus in a negotiation, reframing the information in the context of a loss has more influence than a straight forward gain-oriented statement.

In the context of Postcop, Prakash framed his offering in a loss frame. "Without this equipment, you stand to lose about INR 5 Crores of market revenue on an annual basis." The same sentence in a gain frame of reference would read as "With this equipment, you can add INR 5 Crores of additional revenue of on an annual basis." But that wouldn't have been much effective.

Some examples of framing using loss aversion:

- "Offer from our competitors does not give you A, B, C benefits" rather than "we give you A, B, C"
- "Your business will suffer if you do not implement this strategy" rather than "you will gain by implementing this strategy"
- "If you can't do this now, you will lose the chance to get free products worth INR 5000" rather than "If you do this now, you get a chance to get free products worth INR 5000"

This psychological tool can also be used in a positive sense. A study conducted to sensitize smokers of the risk of cancer used this tool and gained significant breakthroughs. Instead of saying "you will live longer if you quit smoking", the study reframed it as "you will die sooner if you don't quit smoking."

Dhananjay leaned back in his chair and stared at the checkered ceiling. A long silence. He locked his fingers behind his head and stretched his legs. "Yes, you are right in a way. The market is expanding and we have to act now. But again the expenses are frozen and it will be really difficult to convince management."

Prakash leaned forward and mirrored, "convince management?"

Dhananjay brought down his arms back on the table. "Yes, it is year-end close and we are moving towards settling the books. And last moment changes will require management's approval."

"So, it seems that if and *only if* management approves, you can still go ahead with the purchase. So, there might be a chance of presenting the proposal to the management." Prakash rehashed.

"In a way, yes. We can push it, but have to show a significant impact without which management may not agree to signing this so near to year-end closing. Plus, your quotation of INR 24 Lakhs is not a small number. It will require significant financial juggling to accommodate if management agreed to pass your proposal."

"Thank you so much for considering to present the proposal to management. We can assure you that the machine SRX100FC outlined in the proposal is one of the best in the industry right now. Prativa Engineers have been manufacturing this machine line for the past 10 years. Our highly skilled technicians ensure that the machines are calibrated to perform at their peak giving you a low maintenance high output experience for years to come. We have one of the strongest supply chains for procuring the best grade steel which gives these machines extraordinary durability. Plus, all our machines are coated with a proprietary rust-proof solution which ensures that even during rainy seasons or damp conditions, the machines do not degrade in any way. We are an ISO certified organization and each machine goes through a 51-point stringent testing process before getting deployed. Additionally, the SRX100FC works on a specially designed inverter technology which ensures that your electricity consumption for this machine is cut down by 15%. Here is the industry survey data that we have gathered over the past few years which shows how our machines outperform industry standards and provides cheaper and consistent productivity wherever they are deployed."

Prakash pulled out a binder with the survey results and handed it over to Dhananjay.

STRATEGY 3: PROVIDE REASON AND JUSTIFICATION FOR YOUR DEMANDS

A hallmark study conducted by Ellen Langer along with Arthur Blank and Benzion Chanowitz in 1977 changed our perception of human behavior. The study was conducted in a library where the researchers switched off all copy machines except one. As a result, this led to long lines getting formed on that single available copier. Then one of the research associates would walk to the person in front of the line and try to cut her. The associate would then put forth a simple request to the person:

1. Version 1 (request only): "Excuse me, I have 5 pages. May I use the copy machine?"
2. Version 2 (request with a genuine reason): "Excuse me, I have 5 pages. May I use the copy machine, because I'm in a rush?"
3. Version 3 (request with a bogus reason): "Excuse me, I have 5 pages. May I use the copy machine, because I have to make copies?"

If you notice carefully, version 3 was a bogus reason. You would obviously be in line for the copy machine because you have to make copies. There cannot be any other reason. This reason did not contain any new information. However, surprisingly, the researchers found that Version 3 performed significantly better compared to Version 1 and equally well compared to Version 2. The results?

1. Version 1: 60 percent of people let the researcher cut in the line.
2. Version 2: 94 percent of people let the researcher cut in the line.
3. Version 3: 93 percent of people let the researcher cut in the line.

Surprising? Yes, human psychology works in amazing ways. We are hardwired to give in to demands or requests which will help build relationships. This is especially true if the counterpart feels that the

Influencing Strategies

demands being made are being justified and the person asking for it is providing some reason for it.

Negotiators can use this strategy by supplying a reason for their demands, not only financial ones but other nonmonetary demands as well. It helps to improve the chance of your demands getting met. It should be in the form "I am asking for this because…." Additionally, to strengthen your reason follow it up by data points to show that what you said has been proven. Some examples:

1. "I am asking for a leave of 7 days because I have to go and meet my mother and take her for a medical checkup. Here are the doctor's prescriptions"
2. "I want you to come to the office on this Sunday because we are behind the delivery schedule. Here is an email from the client which says that if the project is not getting delivered on time, they can sue for damages."
3. "I want a discount of 15% on this product because that is my budget. I have studied the market and it shows that what I am asking for is a reasonable price."

Dhananjay carefully scrutinized the survey data taking mental notes of certain points. "The data points are decent, but that is anticipated given your experience in the industry. INR 24 Lakhs is still a large amount of money. I have been in purchasing for more than two decades. I know for sure that these decisions will not be passed easily. Also, you have to work out a discount to make the deal better. There are competing products which we can get at a lower price. An investment of this size will require us to be doubly sure before we can go ahead."

"Sir, we understand where you are coming from. It seems to be a bold decision for you to make. We are confident of the quality of our machines. If you look at the industry survey data that I have given you, you would notice that in a competing product you will lose out on the proprietary rust-proof solution that can increase your maintenance cost by 10% annually. You will also lose out on the energy savings that is clearly highlighted here," Prakash flipped over a page on the survey data and pointed to the specifics. He employed Strategy 2, i.e., Highlight potential losses rather than potential gains again.

While Dhananjay was going through the data, he lowered his tone and asked, "Would it be fair for the company to lose out on the growing market opportunity?" sneaking in a perfectly worded 'No' question punched with loss aversion.

Dhananjay looked up, "No, we wouldn't want that." He paused and then added "But you have to give us some discounts."

Prakash had rehearsed the entire flow of today's conversation. He knew exactly where and how to put the concessions he had planned. He said, "Sir, since you are a valued customer for us and we are looking for long term relationships, we will try to give you free maintenance for two years with this deal. I will personally speak to my boss and arrange for this clause to be added to the contract. It will be my responsibility to get you this."

Dhananjay smiled, "Okay, speak to your boss and let me know. By the way, what other companies do you supply to?"

"We are supplying to Sriram Industries, Avani Processing Plant and many more." Prakash pulled out his tablet and pulled up a video, "Please have a look at this video. This machine was installed in Sriram Industries last month and operations have started." After which he proceeded to show him clippings from other factories where these were installed and testimonial videos both from Company heads as well as technicians, engineers and workmen who operated the machines.

STRATEGY 4: CORROBORATE WITH SOCIAL PROOF

Social Proof is the idea that people will adapt their behavior according to what other people are doing. The principle says that we think that something is right if everybody else thinks it is right. People are persuaded more by the action of others than by any other proof we can offer. When you hear teenagers saying, "Dad! Everyone is going for the party!" that is when you know you are getting played on using social proof. Social proof has been in use for a long time in the marketing and advertising domain. Even canned laughter in television to increase the perceived "funniness" of a television show is using social proof.

Social proof is very effective in times of uncertainty and when similarity is evident. When a person is unsure of what his behavior should be in a situation, he will often look at others for clues as to what behavior will seem correct. During such times, providing case studies or precedence of how your solution worked will help to solidify the counterpart's resolve. A brilliant way to use Social Proof when you are trying to rent out your property is to schedule all interested tenants within one specific hour to create a buzz.

Negotiators can use social proof to nudge the counterpart into making quick decisions. Social proof can help to remove indecision to a great extent and lead to quicker resolutions. Some examples of social proofs:

1. A consulting firm provides a limited range of dates to potential clients for their first meeting citing a lack of available slots.
2. Testimonials and Interviews from previous clients; and large Subscriber base on Social Media.
3. Making customers wait in a big line outside the shop or a restaurant.

The relationship between Postcop and Prativa Engineers started a year back, when Prakash had first got in touch with Postcop. Through a reference, he had come to know that Postcop needed a downstream conveyor belt. Dhananjay was the Assistant Director of Purchasing at that time. This was a small project worth INR 2 Lakhs, but it was necessary to start building a relationship with Postcop.

Though the conveyor belt project was a small one, it was not simple. It had complications and specifications that their competitors were unable to provide. Prakash deployed the best engineers to the problem and devised a customized solution. This put Prativa Engineers in their good books and Prakash and his team were appreciated by Postcop's senior management. Over a period of time, Prakash had been deepening his relationship with Dhananjay working with him and the Floor Managers to ensure the smooth running of the conveyor belt. Their requests for servicing and maintenance were prioritized and handled personally by Prakash's team. In all his years in the company, he had learned that it takes a lot of tenacity to get large value orders from clients. And that you cannot get a substantial order without first demonstrating your expertise through small value orders.

STRATEGY 5: DEPLOY THE 'FOOT-IN-THE-DOOR' TECHNIQUE

The 'Foot-in-the-Door' Technique is a strategy used to persuade people to agree to a certain request based on the idea that if the counterpart has agreed to an earlier smaller request they are significantly more likely to agree to a later, much larger request; one which they wouldn't have agreed if asked outright.

Why do people agree to the subsequent larger request? Because once someone has committed to an initial request, they are more psychologically committed to agreeing to the later request. The motivation behind this is that people try to justify past decisions and preserve consistency in their actions. Postcop already had given a go-ahead signal to Prativa for a smaller project and they were happy with the work, so this time when Prativa had pitched for the much larger project, they were more eager to hear them out fully and more bound to honor.

Influencing Strategies

As negotiators, we have many opportunities to use this strategy – not only in sales but also in other areas like conflict resolution, creating political alliances, or selling mobile applications. Some examples of 'Foot-in-the-door' technique:

1. A country asking for a small favor to another country, before asking for a much larger favor involving key socio-economic elements.

2. A political candidate asks people to wear a badge to promote his campaign and then later asks them for campaign donations.

3. Ecommerce websites or e-mailers show the previous products you have brought and then promote new more expensive products.

4. Getting the counterpart to agree to a minor point in the agenda before moving onto larger more significant points, which otherwise would have been outrightly rejected.

The INR 2 Lakhs order had sealed Prativa Engineers as a reliable vendor for Postcop. Their expertise was proven and Dhananjay also got a taste of the quality Prakash and his team could deliver. So, when Postcop asked Prativa Engineer for an RFP for this new machine, he wasn't surprised. But he had a bigger plan. He was fully prepared to influence Postcop to take a decision in his favor.

Prakash knew that Dhananjay was a veteran in purchasing. He would always be asking for more discounts, playing them against competitors and asking for additional features. Prakash's strategy for this new order was to inspect, shock and moderate.

After the initial meeting with Dhananjay, engineers from Prativa had come down to understand the detailed technical specification of Postcop's requirements. They did a thorough analysis of safety requirements, electrical requirements, requirements for cabling and deducting equipment, foundation and support structures, leveling and alignments of the proposed installation area.

Once the engineers submitted the data, Prakash's idea was to shock Postcop using a very high-value request which he knew would anyways be rejected by Dhananjay. He prepared a presentation around the most expensive fully automatic imported machine he had for this category and showed the proposal to Dhananjay. It was valued at INR 72 Lakhs. Without a doubt, the proposal was rejected.

Following close to the heels, he was ready with the second proposal which outlined a moderately priced Indian-made automatic machine with similar specifications. Dhananjay got hooked into the second proposal.

STRATEGY 6: EMPLOY 'DOOR-IN-THE-FACE' TECHNIQUE

The Door-in-the-Face (DITF) compliance-gaining tactic occurs when an outsized request, likely to be rejected, is followed by a comparatively reasonable request that is granted. Robert Cialdini, an eminent psychology and marketing professor at Arizona State University conducted an experiment to find out how to increase compliance to requests. He and his research associates posed as workers from a juvenile detention center and started asking random passers-by whether they would spare some time and accompany a group of juvenile delinquents to the zoo. As expected people were taken aback by this extreme request and only 17% agreed to the request.

Then they changed their approach and asked passersby if they would be willing to serve as a counselor for the detention center for two hours every week for three years. And again as expected everyone rejected this outrageous request. Then the researchers quickly followed up this request with another proposal saying if they can't serve as a counselor will they be willing to accompany a group of juvenile delinquents to the zoo. This time 50% agreed. Three times more people complied in the second case compared to the first case for the exact same question.

Why? Because one, when we retreat from an outsized request and ask for less, the counterpart views this as a concession and feels bound to reciprocate it. And two, the contrast effect – the final request in the second case (accompanying juveniles for one day) seemed more favourable compared to the first request (serving as counselors for three years).

Negotiators can use this technique to anchor their counterparts to requests and get them to bend as per their requirements. Make an initial extremely high offer and immediately follow it up with a moderate offer. Some examples:

1. "This product is worth INR 15000, but we have a special discount going on and you can get it for just INR 3000.

2. Union leaders make very high demands to the management and follow it up by much moderate requests.

3. "We need a donation of INR 100,000 to maintain this program, but all I am asking you is for INR 10000 to keep it going for the next few months."

Foot-in-the-door and Door-in-the-face may appear contradicting but they appeal differently to the human mind. Think that you are visiting a clothing retailer to buy a suit. The attendant shows you a branded and expensive suit which you immediately reject. Then she follows this up with a moderately priced suit and urges you to try it on. Because of the contrast effect, the second suit will appear more reasonable. This is the Door-in-the-face technique. Then later as she is informing you about the suit quality and features, she asks you to do a trial. You wear it, test it out, look at the fittings and comfort level. Then once you are done with the trial, the salesperson has a better chance of convincing you to buy the suit. That is the Foot-in-the-door technique.

Also there is another small difference: A Foot-in-the-door technique requires that enough time has been given to the person to experience the first request. Hence, some amount of time has to pass between the first request and the second request. However, the Door-in-the-face technique requires that the second request be made immediately following the outsized first request.

Dhananjay was finishing up the testimonial videos. He signaled to Prakash that they break for coffee before continuing the meeting. "Let's break for some coffee."

Prakash's conversation was going exactly as planned. Some time back, he had told Dhananjay regarding the free maintenance clause that he was giving as a concession. He knew that the maintenance clause can be easily added from their side. He already had approval from his boss. But, he also knew that Dhananjay would be asking for more discounts. He wanted to keep the pricing same and only concede on other terms and freebies.

With Dhananjay not there, he called his boss, "Things are going as per plan here. We have managed to convince Postcop to commit to the product. Dhananjay would require approval from his management to close the deal before the year-end. I would need your help on that. And as we had discussed, Dhananjay asked for discounts, so I have offered him free maintenance like we discussed. But, my gut tells me he is going to ask for more. So, I will be gradually adding on the spare part assistance for 1 year. If he persists more, we can add the tranche payments option also to it. Any help required, I will give you a call." And he hung up.

Dhananjay came back with coffee. "I just spoke to my management over call; this deal still seems costly for us, especially being year-end."

Prakash was ready. "Sir, we have offered you a very competitive price for the machine. This is one of the best and most efficient Aluminum Container Manufacturing Machine in the market," he continued outlining the features of his product once again and how they have helped increase the production capacity of their client with considerable energy savings.

Then he added, "Sir, we have already added the two-year maintenance contract to the deal. However, we are committed to your business. And we would like to keep working with you for a long time. Can I speak to my boss and see if we can add the spare parts assistance for you?"

He got up, walked out and pretended to speak to his boss. Then he came back and said, "My boss will take this up with our Managing Director and push for free spare parts assistance for one year. This will cost us a good amount per year and we have to absorb this expense." He emphasized this point, "A free spare parts assistance at such a late stage will add to our budgets significantly. But we want to show our commitment to the deal and we know that spare parts assistance will lower your cost of operations to a great extent."

Prakash continued, "Sir, we have a big task ahead of us to convince our Managing Director for this additional spare parts assistance. We have to show him that the deal has moved. Can you give us an in-principle commitment to meet your management by the following Friday?"

Dhananjay picked up the phone and dialed the Company Secretary. A few minutes into the discussion, he smiled at Prakash and nodded. Agreed. Prakash had got the appointment with Postcop's management.

The tranche payment option was kept in reserve. If Dhananjay or his management pushed further, Prakash would get his boss to call him in two or three days with the final concession.

There are 3 strategies that Prakash used back-to-back. Let us take a look at all three.

STRATEGY 7: SEPARATE THEIR GAINS BUT COMBINE THEIR LOSSES

People prefer getting gains in installment and hearing losses in one shot. To ensure that the impact of the gains the counterpart is getting is maximized, it is advisable to break up the total gains into smaller wins and deliver on a piecemeal basis to the counterpart. People respond better to multiple good news and gives them multiple reasons to smile. If you have the ability to make multiple concessions, do not make them all at once. If you have rewards or benefits to offer, share them over a period of time.

Prakash had three concessions that he could give to Dhananjay. One, the free maintenance assistance, the spare parts arrangement and the tranche payment. He gave the first concession – the free maintenance assistance – early on when the client was asking for it. The second one – spare parts arrangement - he gave well into the discussion. And he held back the third option – tranche payment – to be used later by his boss.

There were no losses or bad news that Prakash had to share here. But if in a negotiation if there are multiple bad news to be shared, then share all of them in one shot. People will feel lesser pain if they receive all bad news or losses in lumpsum. If you want to demand concessions from the counterpart, make all demands at once comprehensively. If there are costs or obligations to impose, combine into one and impose.

Some examples of separating their gains:

1. If you want to give discounts to clients, break the total amount under different headers and deliver them in piecemeal basis over the course of the discussion.
2. If you have to give the good news to your boss that the project finished before the deadline and also within budget, give the two good news on different days.

Some examples of combining their losses:

1. If the project has overshot the budget and running late, give both bad news in a single shot.

Influencing Strategies

2. If you have to increase the pricing for a client and cut back on freebies, send them one consolidated email with all the details.

STRATEGY 8: STAMP THE CONCESSIONS

In negotiation, never assume that your actions will speak for themselves. Reciprocation may be required in many negotiations where the counterpart has to concede something in response to your concessions. But it may so happen that the counterpart does not notice you are making the concession. Or, the counterpart undervalues the concession you are making to get the deal or ignore the concession to escape feelings of reciprocation. To ensure that they remember the concession and the difficulty it is causing you, always stamp the concession. Stamping the concession means that instead of simply giving away or moderating your demand, specifically point it out that the concession is difficult for you.

Prakash when putting out the second concession on the table outlines that it will have a significant cost to Prativa Engineers and that the company will have to absorb the costs to make the deal work. He emphasized the point to ensure that Dhananjay takes notice.

To make the stamping work, there are three steps:

1. Let the counterpart know how much it is costing you to make the concessions. By stating explicitly, you ensure that they cannot ignore you.
2. Emphasize the benefits to the other side. Show that by making the concession, you are committed to getting the deal done and how it will help them.
3. Don't concede quickly. Spend time sticking to the initial deal and explain how the deal is beneficial to both sides. Only after severe requests by the counterpart release the concessions one by one.

Some examples of stamping the concessions:

1. "Sir, this project is absolutely a priority. Though coming on weekends to office is very difficult, I am asking my parents to come down to my place for this weekend and take care of my kids while I come to the office and work on the project."
2. "It is impossible to increase the wages by 5%. We can do a 1% increase but even that is costly and will impact the finances of the company significantly."

STRATEGY 9: DEMAND RECIPROCITY

Never give a free meal to the counterpart. Demand something specific in return whenever you are making concessions. This ensures that the cycle of reciprocity is maintained and that the counterpart also understands your pain points. No one understands what you value more than you do. If you don't speak up and voice your demands, the counterpart will give you what they feel your concession was worth and what is convenient to them. Ensure that your demand is specific.

Prakash gives out the concession of spare parts assistance and then asks for the specific favor – a meeting with the management by Friday. That is a specific demand in lieu of the concessions he made. He wanted to make it clear that getting that extra concession will take much effort on his part and he wanted Dhananjay to return the favor by fixing an appointment with Postcop's management.

Some more examples:

1. "This was difficult, but we were able to accommodate a discount in the pricing for this project. With this better pricing, we sincerely feel that you may be in a better position to extend the project deadlines by 3 months."
2. "Our budget was INR 1000 for this purchase. However, after discussing internally, we may be able to squeeze in another INR 100 for this purchase. Can you deliver the product two days in

advance?"

With a commitment by Dhananjay to get Prativa Engineers a meeting with their management, Prakash's work for the day was done. He had successfully stopped the deal from stalling. Better still, he had got themselves to the final stage of approval. Careful planning and strategizing how the discussion will flow had ensured that Prakash can navigate any objections from Dhananjay and yet influence him to take a step forward in their favour.

All in half a day's time. Not a bad return on time invested. Prakash had since been promoted as the All India Sales Head and to this day remains a good friend of mine.

CHAPTER SUMMARY

Throughout the book, we have discussed on understanding the other side's perspective and investigating into what they want. These discoveries of hidden interests, priorities and constraints allow you to create more value through the deal. But that is not the whole story. You would sometimes want to "sell" your story and persuade them to see your side of the deal. Influencing skills not only help you create value for yourself but also does expectation settings which can be useful to close the deal effectively. Here are the key takeaways from this chapter:

- Provide a symbolic unilateral concession to initiate the cycle of reciprocity.
- Emphasize potential losses rather than potential gains. People are more sensitive to loss oriented frame of reference rather than a gain oriented frame of reference. A potential loss gets them to wake up and take notice.
- Follow up your demands with a proper reason and back-up with data. It helps to tell your counterpart why your demands are reasonable.

- Share how other similar parties have benefited from the deal – share social proof as much as possible.

- Get a foothold with the counterpart with a smaller request first. If they agree to the initial request, they are more likely to agree to a larger request later on.

- Use the contrast principle to get your counterpart to see value. Present a massively large demand which you are certain would get rejected and follow it up immediately with a relatively moderate request.

- If there are concessions to be made, break them into smaller items and share them over a period of time. Don't share them all at once. However, do the reverse for losses. Combine losses and share all in one go.

- Let your counterpart know what you have made a concession. Tell them explicitly.

- Never give something without asking something in return. It shows that you have conceded and it is your counterpart's turn to do so.

PRICE IS JUST A PERCEPTION

Never assume what you feel is a good price cannot be bettered at all. Price is just a perception and like any other perception, its perceived value changes depending on how you look at it.

Some years back, my office was exploring to purchase new technology for client management. Our existing technology was not able to keep up with the increasing data loads. So, we decided to invest in new software. It was not an immediate need. The existing software could power us for some more time, but we wanted to start our search early to prevent this *want* from becoming an urgent *need* and take away our negotiating power.

Our administration head went through some thirty-odd vendors, compared their offerings, their reputation, testimonials from existing clients and finalized one vendor which fit all of our requirements. She asked their business development manager Tushar Shaw to meet me at our office.

Tushar Shaw represented Web-IT Solutions, a small-sized firm providing customized and off-the-shelf software for business. They had been in business for over 10 years and had worked across the country with some reputed names. The solution that they had proposed was better than the other offers, had more depth and feel for the end-users and was much faster than our existing software.

After the initial discussion on the product features and delivery terms, we got down to price negotiations. The psychological tools that we described earlier like voiding the mind, mirroring, rehash and acknowledge, dynamic silence, focus questions have done their part to get as much information as possible from Tushar as possible. It has now come down to price.

There are two ways nuances around price negotiation.

One, price negotiation is an area where people experience the most fear and anxiety. By nature, people feel the urge to concede and take whatever price is thrown at them just to avoid negotiating. This is a natural reflex. Negotiations are taxing, but price negotiations are like hell for most.

Two, many people jump into price negotiation right off the bat. That is, if something is not working out in a deal (as a buyer or a seller), there is an issue with the price and that needs to be looked at. The reason price negotiation is one of the last chapters in the book is because price is just a perception. Only if everything else has been settled and other information and value has been extracted from the negotiation, should one get down to price.

Never ever get into price discussion right away in the negotiation. It shifts the focus from what value you can bring to the table to what costs it will entail to get there. And that is a very bad strategy.

The concept of price negotiation is more than back and forth offers and counteroffers. It is about understanding how an offer affects the

Price is just a Perception

other party and what their reaction would be. It is about understanding the emotional undercurrents that are playing out and the psychological thought process that they are having. Whatever plan you might have, whatever number you have in your mind about budgets, if you aren't prepared well, you can be taken for a toss in price negotiations. Everything boils down to planning and knowing yourself.

Coming back to our discussions with Tushar. One thing that we have to understand is that the marginal cost of software tends to go down with every sale. A bulk of the cost for the software is borne upfront during the development and testing phase. After which for over-the-shelf software, each additional sale does not require much overhead. Yes, there are maintenance and updating costs and new feature deployment from time to time. But, once the initial software has been developed, selling to an additional customer does not require much investment. So, we could get away with a low price if planned properly.

BATNA, RV, ZOPA AND EXPECTED PRICE

What should the first offer be?

To understand how to put together the first offer, we have to understand some concepts. The first concept is the idea of BATNA.

BATNA is the short form for Best Alternative to a Negotiated Agreement. Simply put, if the negotiation ends in no deal, what is the best alternative. What should we do if the negotiation ends in an impasse? Without an understanding of BATNA it is hard to know if and when to accept the offer and when to walk away to pursue other options. Keep in mind that BATNA is not what you think is fair or the price that you want to achieve in the negotiation. BATNA is the reality you will face if you do not reach an agreement in the current negotiation.

In our case here, if this particular negotiation with Tushar does not work out at our preferred pricing, we can approach other vendors or simply continue with our existing software.

The next concept is the idea of Reservation Value. Reservation Value is the walk-away point for you in the negotiation. It is the least favorable point at which you will accept the negotiation offer. For a buyer, it would be the maximum they are prepared to pay and for the seller, it is the minimum they are willing to accept.

Suppose you are a buyer and you are negotiating with a seller. You already have negotiated another offer to buy at INR 1000. Is your reservation value INR 1000? Not really, if you know that you can go back and renegotiate a discount of 10% on that. So, your effective reservation value becomes INR 900.

The final concept is that of ZOPA. ZOPA is the short form for Zone of Possible Agreement. ZOPA encompasses all deals that are acceptable by both parties. In effect, it is the space between the seller's reservation value and the buyer's reservation value. If the seller's RV is INR 1050 and the buyer's RV is INR 1200, then all deals falling within this range (INR 1050 to INR 1200) will be considered under ZOPA.

Now with technicalities out of the way, let's look at how to set the first offer.

Find a price that you are willing to pay for the deal. This is called Expected Price. This is different from ZOPA or Reservation Value that we just discussed. ZOPA and RV can guide to this value but will not give a clear understanding of this price. The price that you are willing to pay for will depend on your analysis of your counterpart's BATNA. What are the alternatives that the counterpart has if the deal falls through?

Tushar had quoted us a price of INR 800,000 for the software. Because we knew that over-the-shelf software had low marginal cost to sell, their RV was very low. We could get away with a very low price. Our RV was somewhere around INR 240,000 for the software. However,

Price is just a Perception

during the course of discussion with Tushar through techniques of active listening and focus questions, we discovered that he may have a much lower cutoff internally. His main objective was to make a sale to cover the marginal cost for the software and add a new customer to his pool. As long as he wasn't making a loss on the sale, he would accept a lower bid.

From all this, we figured out we could get away with a bare minimum tag of INR 120,000 for this software.

STEP 1: MAKE THE INITIAL OFFER AT 60-65% OF THE EXPECTED PRICE.

We started the price negotiation. "Tushar, it was great understanding in detail how the software works and the different features. This truly is an excellent product and would be helpful to make our processes more efficient." I let in a brief pause. "However, we are not sure how we can even place this request before you. This was a difficult year for us and we have major budget constraints. We really liked what we saw and found you to be upfront and genuinely interested in helping us, so wanted to check with you before we move onto another vendor. After a meticulous discussion with the managing board, we managed an allocation of INR 78000 for this purchase."

Look at the structure of the request. We build a lot of empathy initially, and anchored his expectation that he can get a sale from us. We followed it up by triggering a loss aversion statement hinting that if things didn't work out with Tushar, we may have to look at other vendors. And then finally dropped the price anchor.

Blood drained out from Tushar's face. He had not excepted such low a number. He tried to recompose himself and fake a smile. What step 1 does is use an extreme anchor to knock off the counterpart from their estimates. Especially if they are rookie. But anchors work on anybody, even experienced negotiators. An anchor is a number that focus the counterpart's attention and expectations. When the counterpart is uncertain about the fair or appropriate price of the deal, they are likely to gravitate towards any number which is thrown into the negotiation.

Tushar wiped his face with a kerchief and centered himself on the chair. "Sir, our software has a lot of features and is easy to deploy. We have built in a proprietary technology that speeds up the processing even with large quantities of data. Plus, we have overhauled the GUI which makes it smooth to use on regular basis. We value your business, however, the price you are asking for is not possible. But since we are beginning this relationship with you, it would be my imperative to assist you to get the best deal. I can look at giving you this software at INR 4,40,000."

Huh! That's almost a 50% drop. My anchor worked. It had rattled the counterpart and got him to make an immediate concession.

STEP 2: MAKE THE NEXT OFFER AT 80-85% OF THE EXPECTED PRICE

"Tushar, thanks for understanding our situation. Your offer is generous, but we are constrained with our budgets. We had made some investments in the last month in expanding our services and we have almost exhausted ourselves. The best we can work out would be INR 102,000. If you can give us the price of INR 102,000; we will make a cheque for you today itself."

Tushar bit his lips. "Sir, we can help with financing the deal. We have tie-ups with banks and NBFCs and they can help with financing at nominal rates. But INR 102,000 is not workable."

I ignored the ultimatum and continued with a sincere deep voice. "See, Tushar, we really like your software and we are keen to purchase it. But, with the current market conditions and being at the end of this year's budget, how can we pay such a steep price?"

The focus question at the end got Tushar into a bind. It was as if I was requesting his help. It was as if I wanted him to guide me how we can work out such a large value payment for the software. We effectively recruited Tushar on our side. Tushar paused trying to figure out what number he had to offer. He was trying to negotiate with himself and present an offer which he felt would be more acceptable to us. "INR 240,000 would be the final offer." He forced out the words. If we weren't prepared, we would have closed out at INR 240,000 as this was our reservation value and still leave money on the table.

STEP 3: MAKE THE NEXT OFFER AT 94-96% OF THE EXPECTED PRICE.

"Thank you Tushar for being with us till now. We understand that you have to work out something back at your office for us. We are constrained by budgets and we then may have to delay the purchase by a few months since we are running short of allocated funds."

We pretended to go through my account statements and budget allocations. Then pulled out a piece of paper and did some fake calculations. After more deliberations, I said, "We can squeeze in another INR 12700 for this software. There you go. Total INR 114,700. We will sign the cheque right away."

Tushar could not believe what was happening. He was at his wit's end. "Sir, let me call my boss." He slid back his chair and stepped out of our office.

Anything that is not a direct no or a walk-out has a probability of working out in our favour. All of Tushar's negotiation weaponry was disabled and he was now super-focused on getting us the price to seal the deal. A good fifteen minutes later he came back. Exhausted. "We can do at INR 120,000 for the software."

STEP 4: MAKE AN OFFER AT 100% OF THE EXPECTED PRICE BUT MAKE IT A NON-ROUND NUMBER

We pulled out the cheque book, paused and looked back at the laptop with the account statements. I let in a long moment of silence. Then said, "I am writing you a cheque of INR 119,880 as that is the last amount in the account right now."

A non-round number always looks more stable and resolute than a rounded number like INR 120,000. A rounded number feels like a temporary placeholder and can be changed anytime. A non-round number feels more solid – something that has come up after a lot of deliberation. People are inclined to assume, true or not, that the negotiator must have researched and gone through piles of data to come up with such a specific amount. A round number, on the other hand, implies that the negotiator is simply ballparking the figure, that is providing a loose valuation based on vague knowledge.

STEP 5: THROW IN A SMALL NON-MONETARY ITEM AT THE END TO SHOW THAT YOU ARE AT YOUR LIMITS

Then we continued, "You have been understanding of our position and helped us through the entire process. INR 119,880 is all we have. However, can you share your card and send me company brochures? We will arrange for them to be sent to some of the other businesses we know. Anyone who would be requiring similar software can contact you directly."

The non-monetary item at the end signifies that you are at your maximum limits and that you have nothing else to concede monetarily. This non-monetary item should be something that is of little value to the other side and of even lesser cost to you.

This is the Ackerman system of Bargaining, a master tool that any and all negotiators must add to their kitty. Why does it work?

Firstly, it uses psychological tools like anchoring, boosting the counterpart's self-esteem and reciprocity. Every step is designed in a

Price is just a Perception

way that the counterpart feels that you are giving a concession and that they need to reduce their offer in return. This way the counterpart feels that they are milking you at every step and hence it massages their ego. However, in reality, you are approaching your desired Expected Price.

Secondly, the extreme anchor shakes the counterpart into coming down to their limits immediately. It is an effective technique to focus the attention of the counterpart on the number you are suggesting and makes them lean heavily towards it.

Thirdly, using rehash and acknowledge wherever possible keeps high levels of empathy. Always be requesting than demanding. That way you come across as non-threatening even when you are saying 'No' to the counterpart's demands. You can use focus questions to get them to bid against themselves.

Finally, a non-round number gives the feeling that you are at your limits. It tells the counterpart that that is the maximum they can get out of you. Throwing in a non-monetary item at the ends also helps this cause.

And thus, we walked away with a brand new software at INR 119,880 instead of the quoted INR 800,000.

Two more inferences regarding this negotiation. One, note that ZOPA and RV gives you a very rational view of the negotiation. It is a logical conclusion of where you can expect your final price to come in. But, because negotiation is inherently stressful and if you can find out the underlying psychology and the emotions, you can close the deal better than you ever thought possible.

Two, never anchor very high or very low depending on whether you are a seller or the buyer. If for example, in this case of software purchase, we anchored the initial price at INR 20,000. Tushar would walked away without making a counteroffer. Why? Firstly, because he would have felt insulted. And secondly, this would not have covered his marginal cost of sales. You have to do background research to find out more about the negotiation, industry standards and typical deals in the industry. Without which you run the risk of distancing your counterpart.

How does the Ackerman model for work for sellers? Use 135%, 115%, 105% and 100% for the price keeping all other things the same.

NEGOTIATING YOUR SALARY

Life is negotiations. And salary happens to be one part of it. Maybe a critical part. So, when it comes to salary negotiations, it is not only entwined with emotions, but people get carried away or become angry or reticent if their salary demands are not met. Suppose you are interviewing with a company and after the preliminary discussions, the interview asks you, "So, if we make a competitive offer now, will you accept it?" What do you do?

Or, you just received an offer from a company that you always wanted to work with. Their work culture is good, they have flexible work hours, plus a lot of learning opportunities. However, the salary is on the lower side. You call up the hiring manager if they can improve the salary. She replies, "We usually don't hire people with your background. But we would be making a one-off hiring with you. This job isn't only about money. Are you saying that you would be rejecting the offer because of the money?"

Or, you have been working in a company for five years. The salary is low but you like the work there. Recruiters are chasing you with offers from other companies where the salary is much better. How do you discuss this with your boss and ask for a raise?

In today's world, people move not only within sectors but across sectors as well. There are a lot of flexibility about who can be hired – people with vastly different work experience, salary history, backgrounds or strengths are present in the employee pool. This makes it a whole lot difficult for companies to maintain a standard package for employees.

And whenever there is an environment where there is no standard price for an item, or in this case, standard job package, it opens up the field for negotiations. How do you navigate this challenging territory? Look at what Shweta did when she was looking to switch companies.

Shweta Malhotra, aged 36 years, joined our online classes in January 2017. She was the branch manager of a large multinational bank based out of Bangalore. Hardworking and dedicated, she had grown through the ranks. Starting from the Assistant Manager role that she got just after her MBA, she had demonstrated her ability to deliver results again and again. In a recent alumni meet, she found out that a few of her friends who had switched multiple jobs were getting at least 30% more than her current salary. She loved working at this organization, but she deemed that her salary should be on par with others in similar roles.

RULE 1: SEED YOUR BOSS'S MIND

Salary negotiations do not start when you walk into your boss's cabin on the discussion day. It starts weeks or sometimes months ahead. Negotiating a salary takes patience. Think of it as preparing for a feast rather than an evening snack. You run the danger of sounding too pushy if you pile it up on the last day. The right way to negotiate your salary is to put the notion of what you want way before the negotiation starts. It's like seeding. You insert the idea into your boss's mind and let it germinate. Let your boss start thinking about it and tossing the idea in his brain. The more space this notion of increment takes up in your boss's mind, the more you stand to gain. Like a friend of mine did. When he was at an event after-party that his company had thrown for its clients, he mentioned how some of his friends in other sectors were earning more than what he was currently drawing. Plus, that they had more leaves. His boss later gave him a raise close to what he asked for.

Shweta bumped into her boss one day when she was speaking

sharply on the phone. After her call ended, her boss asked, "Who was that? Seems to be disturbing you a lot."

"Yes, that was a recruiter. They had got my number from somewhere and have been since then pestering me for switching my career. They even suggested a 40% hike in salary." Never let a good opportunity pass. Shweta seized that moment to seed her boss' mind with her expectation.

There is a disclaimer to this rule. Always let your boss know that he can get you. That is, if he fights for you to get you something, you will stay with him. Nobody will get you anything if they suspect that you're going to walk away anyway. If ever he feels that you want to start a bidding war with a competing organization or use the hike in your current organization to negotiate with other companies or vice-versa, this will back-fire.

RULE 2: RESONATE WITH YOUR BOSS

Just like a football game, you have to play the offense and the defense. After the seeding was done, it was time to play the defense. Which in this case, was to empathize and resonate with her boss. Likeability is very important in negotiating your salary. After all, he would be speaking to you regularly, if not daily. He wouldn't want someone on his team who he doesn't like. It is not only being polite, but also how you handle regular work, handle asking for raise and be persistent without being a jerk. Shweta kept at this point for a few weeks. She broached the idea of some new project ideas for the department and how they would help her boss get more visibility in the system. Remember your success depends on your boss's success in the system. If your boss gets the visibility, you will get what you want.

Shweta added, "Sir, I feel that for the department to be more visible across the organization, we need to take up the new data optimization project and present it to the country head. We have resources to deliver the project and show significant time saving for the bank operations. This way, we can save on man-hours not only for us but for all branches across India." Showing empathy and resonating is key in any salary negotiation. As the negotiations progresses, you will see how resonating get deployed all through the discussion.

RULE 3: NEGOTIATE MULTIPLE FACTORS SIMULTANEOUSLY

Finally, it was that day when her boss called Shweta to his cabin for the year-end discussion. After the elementary conversation was over, instead of moving to salary and increments, Shweta broached the idea of getting a new designation and incorporating flexibility in her work schedule. Jumping into salary would sound too transactional and pushy. She wanted to soften her asks by discussing about non-monetary items.

Negotiating a job offer is not the same as negotiating your salary. A job is much more than just salary. You should be willing to look across the spectrum and explore various options that could be beneficial to both yourself and the company. I know of people who have negotiated one week of additional leave each year for vacations, access to training programs within the company and pushed for preferred shifts where available.

"Shweta, I know you have been with the company for many years now, twelve to be precise. You have shown expertise in your own work and can handle work with relative ease. For flexibility, I don't think I will be able to grant you that. We have strict timings that branches need to operate and you need to be present to take care of the unit." Having said 'No' to Shweta's request, her boss guarded himself and was more open to grant something in return.

"But, I can get you an additional week off yearly for you. It is in my control and I can approve that. Plus, we can look at giving you a new designation but I have to speak to the country head for that. I cannot promise anything, but I can pitch and see his response."

Shweta continued, "Thank you so much, it means a lot to me. I am looking forward to your support for the new national projects that we are picking up. It will help our branch position itself strongly on the national level."

RULE 4: LET YOUR BOSS GO FIRST

If you have done a good job till now with seeding and resonating, your boss would have already worked out some numbers in his head. He would not have come prepared to the table without some numbers ready with him.

"Shweta, we are looking to give you a raise of 20% this year."

Shweta acknowledged her boss's statement but did not say yes or no to the offer. She started speaking on items about how they could work together on improving efficiency in the department. She knew that whatever number her boss says that would mostly be on the lower end of what his range. Instead of directly challenging or accepting the offer, she wanted to let her boss go through the pain of renegotiating in his head, "Did I give something less? Should I increase? Is it too low?"

The more time you give to your boss, the more he will try and overcompensate. There is a difference in how your boss would handle the salary negotiation and how an HR would do it. An HR would be going through hundreds of job negotiations every year and maybe indifferent to your specific needs. But your boss would be more willing to go the extra mile to keep a good resource.

Shweta had anchored her boss at 40%. She never expected him to give a 40% hike. But, something at 20% was what she was expecting. With her boss's initial offer at 20%, she knew she could push her boss some more. Again, if she wasn't prepared with the negotiation, she would have folded then and there. But as the saying goes, never leave money on the table. She wanted to explore further.

There is a cautionary note to this rule. Prepare and be mentally ready for a low number from your boss. You have to resist the initial anchor and keep aiming high. Keep your focus on your expected number.

RULE 5: RECRUIT YOUR BOSS AS YOUR MENTOR

Ben Franklin Effect is a psychological phenomenon which states that a person who has already done a favor for you is more likely to do another favor to you than if they had received a favor from you. Put differently, if the other person helps you in some way, he is more likely to have a better impression of you than if he hadn't helped you or if you had done him a favor. It happens because of cognitive dissonance. Simply put, when you ask your boss for a small favor and he does that favor for you, your boss will start liking you more. So what better way to do this than to get your boss invested in you.

How does the Ben Franklin effect work?

1. You ask someone (who is not a friend) to do you a favor.
2. They agree to do it, for whatever reason seems fit to them.
3. Their mind starts looking for a logical justification.
4. Their mind attempts to match their attitude towards you with the favor they just did.
5. It "reinterprets" the favor and concludes that you're viewed positively.

Shweta asked her boss, "Sir, I am looking for some guidance on charting my career in this company for the upcoming future. I would like to have you as my mentor and guide me." And then she proceeded into a long discussion on how she can grow her career within the organization.

I remember having done something similar after my selection during MBA placements. I did not knowingly do it - it was an instinctive action. But something that left an impression even years into the job. After the job offer had come through, we got allocated to the different locations within the company and was given the contact details of my would-be boss. Just before joining I called my would-be boss and asked him this one question, "How should I prepare to become successful in the company?" I even forgot the discussion. Years later when I quit the job and on the day of farewell, I was told by this same boss (someone who had by then grown leaps and bounds in the organization) that it was the first time he had ever heard someone asking for mentorship even before joining. And that had left a mark on him. If you are a college graduate looking to get a strong footing with your boss, ask this question and see the game change.

All of a sudden during the discussion, Shweta's boss said, "The maximum I could go is 25%. That's the maximum."

Shweta, as a trained negotiator ignore the ultimatum and began telling him how this increment would help her kids live a more comfortable life and help them get into a good school. She went on to cite that the schools have hiked their fees and that the new school had higher fees. As we have seen in influencing strategies, giving a justification for your ask always helps the cause, especially if you can back it up with data.

Then she added, "Sir, I am asking you and only you for your support. Would it be a challenge for you to help me with a 30-35% increment?" His boss's body language changed. He hadn't expected that. After some discussion about how the bank is going through difficult times, he countered with 27%. Shweta again did not respond with 'Yes' or 'No'.

Whenever you want to anchor someone on pricing, and you do not want to look too demanding, throw a range. If softens the blow. The counterpart would get anchored by the higher number in the range, and yet feel that he has the flexibility and control to decide the final number. Expect always that the counterpart will come at a number at the lower end of the range.

After some more discussion, Shweta's boss countered with 29%. He was negotiating against himself in his mind. Shweta was now close. She now wanted to use the opportunity to she wanted to strengthen the bond with her boss. She was happy with the hike she got. She didn't want to push further.

"Sir, I am grateful to you for guiding me all through these years. Without your support, it would not have been possible to grow in the organization. And I look forward to your direction and encouragement to help shape my career in the organization." Ending the discussion on monetary discussions looks too self-serving. She wanted to end on non-monetary terms.

"Sure, Shweta, And I will push for your designation."

And that is how you ace a salary negotiation.

CHAPTER SUMMARY

You would want to hold off bargaining on price as much as possible till the very end moment. Getting into bargaining early undoes the value creation process. But, sooner or later, you get to price negotiation. Price negotiations are inherently risky. One, because for very concession your counterpart makes, they expect you to make a counteroffer. Two, not knowing your counterpart's real margins may make you bid higher or lower than expected. Here are the key takeaways from this chapter:

- Use the Ackerman Bargaining System. Set your desired Expected Price. Make the first offer at 65% of the desired price.

- Make successive offers at 85%, 95% and 100% of the Expected Price. If your counterpart agrees to any amount before you go to 100%, then you have got an even better deal than expected.

- Resonate with your counterpart – rehash and acknowledge their feelings. Use focus questions to get them to bid against themselves and clarify their position.

- End the bargain with a non-round number and also offer a non-monetary item to show that you are at your limits.

- Salary negotiations are not a one-day match. It requires days and sometimes weeks of preparation. To start the process, seed your boss's mind with an effective anchor and justification for your demand.

- Use empathy and acknowledge your boss's feelings. Likeability is important. Your boss should like you to give you a raise.

- Negotiate multiple factors simultaneously. Remove the focus from salary and move onto non-salary terms like leaves, flexibility, designation, etc.

- Let your boss go first. Let him state what number he has in mind. This may be lower than your expectation, but remember not to get anchored low during this step. Use focus questions and ask him how you can help to get the department or the company to the next level.

- Recruit your boss as a mentor and seek his advice on making your career path in the company. Keep the discussions focused on non-monetary factors and let your boss come up with the salary numbers. Throw in a range if you have to give a number.

APPENDIX

The most common and costly mistake that negotiators can make is to not prepare for the discussion. Most negotiators fail not because they prepared less but because they didn't prepare at all. Negotiation is thought of as an art form rather than science, and people want to ace the game at the table. This faulty interpretation of negotiation as "all art and no science" is costly and can derail the best of negotiators. Negotiations can stress out even the finest. And the less you prepare the more you stand to lose. A prepared negotiator can gain up to 10 times more than an unprepared one.

On the flip side, some negotiators get into an overload of preparation and memorize words and phrases exactly how they are supposed to say or ask. This puts them in a bind and removes the flexibility and agility that is required to make negotiations work. Assumption of how the negotiation would go is another mistake to avoid.

This bonus chapter gives an outline regarding how and what to prepare before getting into the negotiation.

And remember. Practice. Practice. Practice.

SALES NEGOTIATION CHECKLIST

Sales negotiation requires a lot of dexterity. From finding out what the customer wants to unearthing objections to getting a commitment for the deal. And oftentimes ends in a hard bargain. In the middle of all these, a salesperson has to withstand all the punches, gatekeepers, customer egos and competitors.

So, how do you go about it? Here is a 7-Step process:

1. Research the Customer's Background

The first step to preparing for a sales meeting is to dig out basic information about the customer.

What does he want?

What are his constraints?

Why this product? Why us?

Who all are the existing suppliers?

Word of caution: Don't overdo this step and spend weeks on researching stuff that you can get from the customer in ten minutes over a face to face discussion. This step is to get a generic idea of the broad factors that may come into play during the negotiation.

2. Zero in on your Goal

The second step is to figure out what you want from the deal. Step back to look into the bigger picture. The aim of this step is to prevent going into a bargaining mode.

Is it purely monetary or has additional elements to it? Like a Foot-in-the-Door sale?

What is your goal from this discussion?

Figure out your BATNA and your customer's BATNA. What if the deal falls through? Do we have to get this sale? But don't focus on your BATNA too much. Instead find out the Expected Price.

How much do you expect? Get a range and focus on the higher end of the range. It will anchor your mind and help you get the best possible deal.

3. List down the Focus Questions

List down a list of focus questions you can ask to unearth more information. There may be a lot of play behind the scenes. There may be deal killers which if not identified can cause the deal to fall through. Get under the skin of the customer and dig out the why behind every what.

Encourage the customer to open up. Consciously prepare to listen actively and use mirrors, rehash and acknowledge to resonate with the client. Use your emotional intelligence to coax the customer to give you more information. Prepare to appear not so perfect.

Broadly we can classify focus questions into two categories:

A. 'Vetting the Process' Focus Questions

Who will be part of the deal-making process?

How long should you expect the negotiation to go before concluding?

Are there any key factors that can derail the sales?

B. Deal Focus Question

What do you expect from the deal?

What problems will it solve?

Why do you want to use our services when you already have a competing vendor providing similar services?

What is the biggest challenge that you face today?

How does this solution fit into the overall objective of the company?

4. List down the Negatives

If this is a cold call, you have just a few seconds before the customer disconnects. The company might feel that hearing your pitch is a waste of their time. Prepare an apology in that line and follow it up with an acknowledgement of their feelings.

If you are meeting face to face, the customer may feel you have a hidden agenda. What are the accusations that the customer can throw at you? Are these common accusations or are these related to your past performance?

Use "I am sorry that …" to diffuse the negative. Make a list of all possible negatives that can come up and address them as early as possible.

5. Frame the No-oriented questions

Don't get to a 'yes' early. Frame some no- oriented questions. Make the customer feel in control of the discussion. Getting to an early 'yes' is a terrible mistake. Let the customer know that you are okay to hear a 'no'. Ensure that at no point the customer feels cornered into making a decision.

Use 'no' to drag out their fears and hidden information. There will be instances when the customer has not thought through the solution. A no-oriented question also helps your customers get a clearer picture of their wants and demands; and in return allows you to know how exactly you can plug in your product or service.

"Is this a bad time to talk?"

"Is it a bad idea to look at how this deal can make some sense in your business and help you improve your revenues?"

"Do you want the company to lose face during security audits?"

6. Don't Close too quickly

Divide your sales call into three phases: The first phase is the Discovery phase where unearth information from the customer using mirroring, active listening and silence techniques.

The second phase is the Commitment phase where you unearth the customers' pain points and how your solution can help with that. Use the rehash and acknowledge technique to ensure that what you have understood is what they wanted to convey; and that they are now committed to what you have to offer.

The third phase is the Implementation Phase where you outline how to go about execution once the deal is closed. We will look at implementation in the next point.

If you close too quickly you run the risk of getting into the bargaining. Practice holding off closing unless it is absolutely required.

7. How to Implement

Implementations are the most commonly overlooked items in sales. A salesperson's job is not only to ink the deal, but also to ensure that the implementation is done. Your reputation as a salesperson always precedes you. In the end, people buy the person not the deal. If implementation is done by a separate team, then the salesperson has to ensure smooth transition and handover between sales and implementation. If during any moment, the customer feels that he is searching in the dark for the right contacts, the relationship suffers and this can have negative repercussions not only on this deal, but on any deals going forward.

What are the implementation challenges that you can face during implementation?

Does the client want an implementation now or later?

Who from the client-side will be responsible for overseeing the implementation?

Use this 7-point checklist every time you go on a sales call. Practice, Practice and Practice. Till it becomes an inherent part of your sales DNA.

ACKNOWLEDGEMENT

Writing a book is tougher than I assumed and more gratifying than I could have ever envisioned. The world has become better not by individualistic approaches but by collective efforts of countless practitioners of leadership and negotiations. From improving the value of interactions to developing deeper and more meaningful relations, they have shown me the path towards success and well-being.

This book would not have been possible without the support of individuals I have interacted over decades, who have helped me form, either consciously or otherwise, the strength to bring out the best in people and develop my inner peace to navigate through the ups and downs in life.

To my family, close friends and colleagues who have given me continuous support, endless encouragement and unwavering bandwidth to keep writing and penning down the ideas that were overflowing. Without their incessant backing, it would not have been possible for me to complete this book and turn into this final form.

A big shout to all the readers who have taken time out to read my books and who has been my core source of inspiration to continue to give my best and push me to better myself every single day. Without your reinforcement and patronage, I would not have taken the step to convert the ideas in my head to this manuscript.

ABOUT THE AUTHOR

Abhishek Datta is an Experienced Entrepreneur and Coach with a demonstrated history of working with small / medium businesses and large corporates in the field of sales and negotiation. With an experience of over a decade of negotiating in business and professional life and having coached thousands of people, he has turned around businesses, influenced professionals and made a difference in the lives of many.

With a dynamic personality, he has sound understanding of needed traits for workplace success and strong ability to coach in improving these skills. He is associated with leading universities and colleges teaching and guiding students and faculty on the latest skills for personal development and accomplishment. He also has to his credit multiple publications including academic papers and research articles in various symposiums and leading newspapers in India.

He is the head of Vivaron Ventures, a consulting firm which helps entrepreneurs, professionals and businesses navigate tough negotiation and sales and empower them to create self-sustaining livelihoods.

For more information on coaching and training, guidance on negotiation and sales, or for contacting the author, please write to datta.ab@gmail.com.

BOOKS BY THIS AUTHOR

ACHIEVERS' PLAYBOOK

We all have dreams. We want to achieve our maximum potential, make a significant difference to the lives of people around us, make a mark in our personal and professional lives and achieve the goals of our life.

We all had these dreams. But then somewhere all of these took a backseat with other not-so-important urgencies ruling every minute of our days. We wanted to creat the impact in our lives but are unable to carve a path for ourselves!

After spending years on finding out the right tool to keep us on track and after reading volumes of books and tracking some of the best brains in the industry, we came up with The Achievers' Playbook.

The Achievers' Playbook is an ultra-modern format which has been carefully crafted after years of research. It has been our companion for the past few years. We have been using it daily to drive us towards our goals and make a positive impact in our lives.

Initially, we opened it up for few friends of ours and they have experienced a many-fold increase in their productivity and satisfaction. So, we decided to open it up for aspiring individuals who want to make an impact in ther lives.

"Life is too short to be little" - Reveal the Achiever in YOU!

This is an experiential book and is available only on request. To request your copy, send an email to datta.ab@gmail.com with a brief about your goals in life and how you want to achieve them.

Achievers' Playbook has been co-authored by Abhishek Datta and Abhirup Banerjee.